Why Do Bad Things Happen?

D1350856

Why Do Bad Things Happen?

GORDON SMITH

HAY HOUSE

Australia • Canada • Hong Kong • India
South Africa • United Kingdom • United States

First published and distributed in the United Kingdom by:
Hay House UK Ltd, 292B Kensal Rd, London W10 5BE. Tel.: (44) 20 8962 1230;
Fax: (44) 20 8962 1239. www.hayhouse.co.uk

Published and distributed in the United States of America by:
Hay House, Inc., PO Box 5100, Carlsbad, CA 92018-5100. Tel.: (1) 760 431 7695 or
(800) 654 5126; Fax: (1) 760 431 6948 or (800) 650 5115. www.hayhouse.com

Published and distributed in Australia by:
Hay House Australia Ltd, 18/36 Ralph St, Alexandria NSW 2015. Tel.: (61) 2 9669
4299; Fax: (61) 2 9669 4144. www.hayhouse.com.au

Published and distributed in the Republic of South Africa by:
Hay House SA (Pty), Ltd, PO Box 990, Witkoppen 2068. Tel./Fax: (27) 11 467 8904.
www.hayhouse.co.za

Published and distributed in India by:
Hay House Publishers India, Muskaan Complex, Plot No.3, B-2, Vasant Kunj, New
Delhi – 110 070. Tel.: (91) 11 4176 1620; Fax: (91) 11 4176 1630. www.hayhouse.
co.in

Distributed in Canada by:
Raincoast, 9050 Shaughnessy St, Vancouver, BC V6P 6E5. Tel.: (1) 604 323 7100;
Fax: (1) 604 323 2600

© Gordon Smith, 2009

The moral rights of the author have been asserted.

All rights reserved. No part of this book may be reproduced by any mechanical,
photographic or electronic process, or in the form of a phonographic recording; nor
may it be stored in a retrieval system, transmitted or otherwise be copied for public
or private use, other than for 'fair use' as brief quotations embodied in articles and
reviews, without prior written permission of the publisher.

The author of this book does not dispense medical advice or prescribe the use of any
technique as a form of treatment for physical or medical problems without the advice
of a physician, either directly or indirectly. The intent of the author is only to offer
information of a general nature to help you in your quest for emotional and spiritual
wellbeing. In the event you use any of the information in this book for yourself, which
is your constitutional right, the author and the publisher assume no responsibility for
your actions.

A catalogue record for this book is available from the British Library.

ISBN 978-1-84850-102-7

Printed in the UK by CPI William Clowes Beccles NR34 7TL

In this life, we may at some point have to face the harsh reality of a friend's or family member's death being thrust upon us, by a car crash, a serious illness or a life taken by another. It's at these moments that we are unable to cope or understand why.

I believe that in this book, Gordon Smith has in his own unique way found a means to give the insight and clarity that could provide assistance to those faced with the untimely departure of loved ones.

Mica Paris

To my father,
who died earlier this year.

Come back,
otherwise my mother will
have the last word!

Contents

Introduction

'Why Do Bad Things Happen?'

A few years ago in Glasgow, some friends sent a lady to me for a reading at the Berkeley Street Spiritualist Church. As usual, they didn't give me any clues about whom she wanted to hear from in spirit. When she came into the small back room at the church my first impression was of someone who had given up caring about the little details of everyday life – something bigger had come along and wrung that out of her. She was a good-looking older woman, but somehow she seemed limp – her hands fell in her lap as though she was barely aware of them and her hair had been well cut but I don't think she'd bothered styling it. Her face was strangely gaunt compared to her body, with eyes like black circles. When you see someone who's so clearly in pain, you just want to reach out and give them a hug, but as a medium you have to remember that that's not what they've come for – they want to hear from their loved ones, not you.

I explained to her that I wanted her just to listen to any evidence I was able to pass on to her from spirit and to let me know if it was right by giving me a nod or saying she accepted it. I knew that if the person she was reaching out to had a message it would come through, but I also wanted to give her proof that it was genuine, to set her mind at rest so she could get the most from this contact with the other side.

Straightaway I began to sense the familiar energy around me that always means there's a spirit trying to come through, so I sent out my first question: 'Who's there?' In return I got the impression of a child, a little girl who can't have been much more than three years old.

When I told the woman in front of me, her shoulders tensed and she nodded. I knew this must be her granddaughter.

'I know I have a little brother and I come to see him,' the little girl said to me. 'Tell Mummy I'm there.'

This was hard for the grandmother to take. She was listening so intensely that without realizing it she was pulling her chair closer to me, wanting to be nearer to the little girl. The child told us that she was with her great-grandfather, and the woman protested, 'He died ages ago. How can he be with her?' but then her face changed and I sensed her relax a bit before she frowned again. I think she understood that it *was* her granddaughter, but now I could see that she was trying to work out how to prove this to another person – presumably the little girl's mother. She wanted more assurances. I was recording the sitting and promised her she'd have the tape to play back and she said, 'Yeah, yeah,' but she was pushing me for more. Sceptics say that the grieving are gullible, but nothing could be further from the truth – they want concrete evidence, not straws to grasp at.

The initial high that I'd got from making the connection to spirit turned darker and I knew that I was about to get a sensation of what had happened to the child. It only lasted a split second. Sitting in my chair in the tiny room I suddenly felt as though I was free-falling through the air, plunging down, and then it was over and I was still in the chair.

'I want Mummy to dream without seeing me falling,' the girl went on. 'I want to be with her and I can't when she sees that.'

When she heard that, her grandmother nodded and wept, and I wondered if I should have been seeing the little girl's mummy too – it sounded as though she was the one who needed real healing from spirit.

I got a sense of worry from the little girl, but only because she clearly knew her mother was suffering and she was trying to get through to her and let her know that she was in a good safe place now.

I hoped the grandmother was getting some comfort from the evidence I was able to give her. When the communication ended, I let her tell me the story.

Her daughter and granddaughter had lived on the third floor of a tenement building on the outskirts of Glasgow and the conditions were pretty poor. The mother was putting aside as much money as she could so that they could move to a better flat, but she was also phoning and writing to the council to try and get them to do some repairs on the building. She was particularly bothered by the windows, which she thought were unsafe. Two years of letters and calls were getting her nowhere and she had a looming sense that there was something wrong about living in that flat with her little girl. Each time she was let down by the council the dread got worse.

She would go out early in the mornings to work as a cleaner and a neighbour would pop round and mind the toddler. One day, two years before the reading, as she was coming home she felt that feeling of dread kick in again and anxiety mounting inside her. As she turned up the path in front of the building, she looked up to see her little girl kneeling on the window sill, banging her hands on the glass, happy to see her, and as she watched, the window flipped open and the child flew out.

She saw her daughter fall and die.

I cannot begin to quantify the horror that that mother must have felt in that instant, or every minute of every day after that when she saw the child fall and die again and again. The grandmother had come to see me because she had been watching her daughter disintegrate. Although she'd been pregnant at the time, she'd split up with her boyfriend and spent lots of the compensation money on building a shrine to her little girl in the cemetery. She was terrified to sleep because she kept having a dream in which she felt her daughter coming closer to her and then the image of the accident played in her head again and she lost the presence of the child. The grandmother felt as though she had lost not just her grandchild but also her daughter, that she was slipping out of reach.

The neighbour who'd been looking after the child was devastated too – how could she have known that the girl would be able to climb up on a bed and then onto the high sill? A pall hung over the entire estate as the neighbours added their grief to the mother's and held their own children closer, thinking what if it had happened to them?

When you look at the way that the consequences of a single action spread out and taint so many lives, you find yourself demanding to know why. Why that child? Why that mother? Why did *anyone* have to go through that? Why do things like that happen every day, all over the world, and how do the people left behind have the strength to pick themselves up and carry on living? Why do bad things happen?

You might throw your hands up and say it's just destiny, but it's more complex than that and it takes a bigger explanation to understand how that terrible accident came about and how, incredible though it might seem, it could be possible for those left behind to find solace.

Many world religions have their own interpretations of destiny, karma, fate, kismet – call it what you will – and I'm not pretending that I'm going to offer up a definitive theological explanation here, or even explain how it works in Buddhism or Hinduism, or predict the future. I'm not a guru. I can only tell you what I know. But I can draw on my experiences as a medium travelling the world and meeting thousands of people who have gone through terrible ordeals and on what I've learned from spirit to try and show you what's helped me and others to live their lives and grow spiritually, whatever life throws at them.

1

'What Is Destiny?'

In 2005 I was in South Africa for a book tour and was asked to take part in a TV show. The producers drove me out to a very grand house in Johannesburg and when we got there they sprang a surprise. Would I give a reading to two women? I agreed and they settled me in front of the cameras on the patio and brought them out.

I knew it was going to be an exceptional sitting the moment it began. A man came through and I understood that he was the husband of one woman and the brother of the other. When I told them, they both burst into tears. I got a sense of water and of drowning, of pressure on my lungs. They confirmed this.

I tried to tell them what I was understanding: 'I get the sense of a man in the spirit world, somebody quite young, I feel, who went over very, very quickly. Does that make sense to you? He's not been that long in the spirit world. I do feel that this was quite a recent thing and I do feel that it was very tragic. I feel a lot of tragedy here for many people.'

Then I saw a little blonde child and the man put his arms round her to show he was looking after her. He told me she was having breathing problems and when I let the sitters know that he promised a lot of healing for her, they looked at each other and I saw understanding pass between them. He also gave pieces of evidence about his love of fast cars and music, confirmed by the two women, who turned out to be his widow and his sister.

As we went on with the sitting, the penny dropped for me. The death of this man had occurred in the Asian tsunami of Boxing Day 2004, only a few months before the day of the sitting. I hadn't made any connection before the sitting began between South Africa and Thailand, where he'd died. The family had been having the Christmas holiday of a lifetime on an idyllic island, staying in a beautiful villa by the beach. The man had died trying to save his father as he was swept away and drowned. The little blonde girl was one of his four daughters, who had recently been ill with a chest condition. He also mentioned how worried he was about his mother, who was grieving badly, blaming herself for what had happened: 'He just keeps saying, "I need to help Mother, I need to help Mother."'

I hope that reading brought healing to his mother, and to the two women in front of me. The cameraman later told me he'd caught the exact moment when the fact that it really was their lost loved one coming through had dawned on them and they had gone from a kind of dull shellshock to joy. That garden was filled with elation as they realized that their family was together and happy in spirit and still part of their lives on Earth.

That was a joy to see, but where it gets trickier is when you take it further and ask yourself what was really going on. Why was that family caught in a freak occurrence like a tsunami? Why did they die *then*? Why didn't it happen to someone else? Were the surviving women chosen to go through this experience? Did *they* have a choice? Could they have done something to prevent it? That's when you get into the big words like 'destiny', 'fate' and 'karma'.

You can't be in my line of work without coming across the big philosophical questions of life. You might think that the real biggie is whether there is life after death, but for any medium or any bereaved person who's known the comfort of a message from a loved one on the other side, it's simple – of course there is, we just have to be open enough to experience the connection we still have with those in spirit, be they Grandma or the dog. Contact with the spirit world is part of our everyday life, whether it comes through a message from a medium at a demonstration with hundreds of people present or just through thinking of someone you've lost and feeling their presence for a split second when you're doing the washing up or stuck in a traffic jam.

But what about those bigger questions of destiny, fate and karma? We tend to divide everything up into 'good' and 'bad' and think of our lives as an accumulation of deeds which go on some sort of karmic balance sheet. It's even in our everyday language, as we say, 'You reap what you sow.' So, do enough of the good and it'll cancel out the bad. Too much high living and fun and you'll be in for a smack down. Do really well and you'll be rewarded with a nice car and a new girlfriend.

Real life doesn't dish out the gifts and the blows like that, though; it seems much more confusing and contradictory. People want to know why they've lost a spouse in an accident when they've lived good lives and always worked for charity, or why their neighbour won the lottery, even though she's never known how to handle money and is up to her eyeballs in debt. It seems as though there's no logic behind it, and it's tempting to think of a spiteful and capricious force hurling down thunderbolts for a laugh. Or to say fate is cruel and karma is a bitch. Yet all the time we're begging Lady Luck to single us out so we can have our time in the clover. Or claiming responsibility: 'Be careful of what you wish for,' or that it's personal fate: 'What's for you won't go past you' – which just about covers everything!

I've known men and women torture themselves with regret over something long since done and dusted because they are convinced that what they did was linked to a greater tragedy. In a way they're seeking control over the suffering that life dishes out. If someone they loved died abruptly in an accident or through violence, they want to know if it could have been avoided and then spiral into 'what ifs'. It also seems to be instinctive for people to want to blame themselves for the suffering that a child has gone through in order to take some of that burden onto themselves.

We like to take responsibility for some things that are nothing to do with us and yet sometimes we try to pretend that things we really *are* responsible for just came out of nowhere. In both cases we make life much harder both for ourselves and for others. And when you consider that this 'fate' or 'karma' covers everything from the drive to work to world wars and global warming, how do you even begin to get a handle on that? You'd go mad if you tried to think through the consequences of every last thing you did, imagining some terrible punishment forever waiting to drop on your head.

In fact we can spend a lifetime struggling to understand how to negotiate this plane of existence and come out the other side with a lighter mind and greater wisdom. There are lots of mental traps that we can fall into or false roads we can take which leave us at a spiritual dead end.

So how can we make it easier on ourselves? Is there any way we can really tell what is our fate and what, if anything, we can do to change it?

2

'What Can Spirit Tell Us about the Future?'

Jean Primrose was a medium whom I was lucky to have as a mentor. I met her in the early nineties when she was in her seventies and a very respected soul in the Spiritualist church. Towards the end of her life she came round to see me and my partner Jim in our flat, bringing a friend who was a few years younger than her. I asked her how they'd met.

'Can I tell them?' she asked Mrs Primrose.

'It's your story,' she said and gestured to her to go on if she wanted to. So she told us.

Several decades before, she and her husband had been trying to start a family. After several miscarriages she was finally able to carry a baby to term, but her longed-for son died before they had even left the hospital. As she was devastated, her husband had to steel himself and deal with the baby's funeral. The officials in charge needed him to name the little boy before he could be buried and he suddenly thought of the name 'Jamie'. He never told his wife that the baby had been given a name.

A year later she was diagnosed with a condition that meant it was impossible for her to have a child and the couple thought they would never have a family. At about this time a friend persuaded her to go to a Spiritualist church where Mrs Primrose was giving a demonstration, but she was sceptical about mediumship and sat right at the back to watch. She was mortified when Mrs Primrose identified her and said that she had a message for her that she would pass on when the demonstration was over. 'This is ridiculous,' she thought, and tried to sneak away at the end, but Mrs Primrose got to the ante-room before she was out of the door and gently apprehended her.

'Have you got a pen and a piece of paper?' she asked her. 'Because you're going to need this information.'

She wrote down the name 'Jamie' and told her, 'This was a baby you lost and this is the date when he died.'

The date was exactly right, which startled the woman, although as far as she knew the baby had had no name.

Mrs Primrose also told her that she would adopt kids. Then she wrote down two telephone numbers and said, 'Keep these and never lose them. I don't know what they are, but I know you will need them in the future.'

The woman tucked them away in her handbag and hurried home. When she got there she went straight to her husband's bureau and searched for the baby's death certificate, and there it was, her little boy's name – Jamie.

Over the next five years she and her husband adopted a boy and a girl and at last had their family. Some 30 years later, when the two children had grown up, they both became interested in finding their birth parents. They asked their mother if she minded and she promised them that she was happy for them to do it. Both started chasing trails of paperwork and making phone calls, but they didn't have any luck. It seemed as though every line of enquiry had been exhausted.

Their mother was chatting about it with Mrs Primrose one day, saying how she wished she could help them, and then the medium remembered the phone numbers. 'I know it's a long shot, but do you still have that piece of paper?' The woman had kept it for decades in a little drawer by her bed. 'Try those numbers,' Mrs Primrose urged her.

I've heard some incredible stories from mediums in my time, but never one as amazing as this: each of those numbers was connected to the birth parents of the adopted children and through them they were able to get into contact with their birth families.

As their mother finished her story, Jim and I stared at Mrs Primrose in amazement and asked her how on earth she could have known. She just looked at her hands.

Her friend asked us, 'How could you disbelieve when you had something like that happen?'

I realized from the earliest messages I witnessed being delivered by mediums that those in the spirit world seemed to have some way of not only knowing what had happened to loved ones in this life since they had passed, but also of predicting their future. It was some time before I had first-hand experience of this and also had the chance to have an explanation from the other side.

One night I was in the Spiritualist church in Somerset Place in Glasgow, taking part in a meditation circle, when the practice I was trying to focus on gave way to an image of Jim in our flat in the Gorbals. He was looking really worried. He was sitting with a friend of ours called Mark, a South African who was living in the UK with his girlfriend Carla. Mark and Jim both played the guitar and I knew they were meeting up that night to have a jam together, but I couldn't understand why Jim was looking so anxious or why I was experiencing that anxiety so strongly.

I came home to find Jim in the flat and asked him how the guitar session went.

'Oh, yeah, it was fine,' he said evasively.

'No, something happened,' I insisted.

'Nothing happened,' he replied.

'Go on, Jim, tell me what happened,' I pushed, but he was having none of it.

The next day I was sitting on the sofa next to Jim having a cup of tea when I was suddenly aware of a build-up of energy around me. After that, as far as I was concerned, I shut my eyes and nodded off, but when I came to later I found Jim looking stunned. He told me what had happened.

I hadn't nodded off, I'd gone into a trance, and one of my spirit guides, Chi, had come through and spoken to Jim.

Everyone has a spirit guide who is there to mediate their experience of spirit, help connect them to loved ones on the other side and aid them in this life. When they work with a medium, guides often have a speciality and in writing this book I've found myself referring again and again to explanations I've been given by Chi, whom I first heard about when I was attending a demonstration by the well-known medium Albert Best. He is the guide who's taught me the most about prediction and destiny, so it was no surprise that he came through at that moment to talk to Jim.

'Yesterday,' Chi said, 'Mark told you his and Carla's visas had run out and there was only one way for her to stay in Britain. He asked you if you'd marry her. He put you under a lot of pressure and in the end you told him you would.'

Jim was incredulous. 'How do you know that? I haven't told Gordon. There's no way he could know that either.'

Chi didn't answer that, but went on, 'You've made a commitment to this woman now, but you won't have to fulfil it. She will be called back to her country before you can go through with it.'

'But how can you know that?'

This time Chi explained, 'By saying yes you stepped onto a new timeline, and by starting it, you made it possible for me to look along that line into the future and be able to tell you some of what will happen.'

'Why will she have to go back?'

'I haven't looked that far along the timeline. Perhaps it's better that you don't know,' said Chi, then he leaned me over and made me pick up a pack of tarot cards that Jim had shoved under the sofa when I came home. He'd been desperately trying to get answers about what would happen in the future.

Chi went on almost playfully, 'If there are 78 cards in that pack and if I have a greater overview in spirit, I can probably predict the next card to come out.'

Then he told Jim what the first card would be and Jim turned it over and it was correct.

Then he did the same thing three times in a row.

'That might look like a trick to you,' he said, 'but

it's not. If the first card is the four of cups, then the rest of the deck will lie like this,' and he went through the whole pack, getting it right each time. 'There are only so many orders for the cards if you begin with the four of cups, so it's just a question of probability.

'If something has begun, then other things will follow it. You predict the future on the basis of what you know in the moment. But if you're a card in the pack, you probably have no idea where you are or which card comes after you. I know that you're worried because you've set off this timeline for marrying Carla, but I've come to tell you not to be. You did this out of loyalty because you thought you would be considered a bad friend if you said no, but in future you should be more careful.'

At that point I came out of the trance and woke up. Jim told me the whole story and I learned about his conversation with Mark for the first time. We both wondered what would happen to cause Carla to go back to South Africa.

We didn't have to wait long to find out: two weeks later Carla's father died and she left the country. We never heard from her or Mark again.

Our lives are full of potential timelines that stretch out in front of us like paths: to choose a life with this person and not that person, to stay where you are instead of taking a job in a new town, even to turn right at a road junction instead of left. You have the potential to live out many different experiences and lives with a huge number of people, although it may feel as though you just follow one linear path. We're all like soap operas, with lots of plots running side by side.

We may step onto several timelines at the same time and we may be unaware that we've even begun one. The act of meeting one person can open up a mass of new timelines, like thousands of fibre-optic cables squeezed together in one wire, or lifetime. Some of these will just burn off or fade away – timelines, like everything we come across in our lives, can develop fully or flourish for a short time and then disappear from our lives. Sometimes we abruptly change direction and find ourselves on a new path with new opportunities and a new future branching out in front of us. We may make a conscious choice to do this or we may just feel an instinct to pursue or avoid a situation.

Sometimes the timelines are interconnected: the more in tune you are with your life, the more you'll see how many lives come together in a network that expands beyond your friends and family to strangers you've never even met.

If a timeline has begun, a prediction can be made or a precognition come through – like the one that Mrs Primrose gave. After losing her son, the woman was on a track to adopt those two children. That's why Mrs Primrose was able to give her the phone numbers that wouldn't make sense for decades. But action is crucial to bring that future into being; if there's just a thought or a wish that something will happen, that future won't be seen.

Now, obviously no one in this world can make predictions to the degree that a spirit can. Spirits can do this because they have a wider vision that looks above and beyond our own narrow limits and because they can look at the complicated map of different choices that an individual can take and calculate the outcome more effectively. But some people in this world can see ahead along a timeline. That's why some psychics were able to predict September 11th – the news was already in the ether and the chain of events that would lead directly to it were already under way.

Obviously even the best psychic doesn't see everything laid out neatly in full colour and detail, and when our loved ones in spirit intervene to pass on news, they rarely try to show us the whole picture. I've often been in the middle of passing on a message when a spirit has let me know something about the fate of the person sitting opposite me, but I pass on this information only if there's something that can be done about it. Very often the spirit world has its own reasons for withholding information.

My good friend Jackie lost her father and asked me to give the funeral service. I was only too happy to do so, as I knew her family well. After church we went back to her parents' house to have a cup of tea and her mum pulled me aside and said, 'At some point, darling – I know it's too soon now – will you do me a reading?' I told her when she was ready she should give me a call and I'd try and get through to her husband for her.

Two weeks passed and Jackie called. 'Will you sit for my mum?'

Out of pure instinct, I said, 'Something's telling me it's not the right time.' I couldn't have told her why, but it just didn't seem right. I wasn't getting a clear signal from spirit.

Another two weeks passed and Jackie rang again. 'Is it time yet?'

'No, I don't think it is.'

'Why? What's wrong? Is something the matter?' I could hear her beginning to get nervous.

'No, I don't think so. It's just one of those times when it's not ready to happen yet.' I tried to reassure her and then we had a chat and that was the end of the call.

A short time later, Jackie's mother died out of the blue. Poor Jackie was devastated and, like her mum, she came up to me at the funeral and asked if I'd give her a reading as soon as possible. Once again, all I knew was that I couldn't do it, although this time something was different: I felt an energy building up, but I had no idea what it meant. It was incredibly hard to turn a friend down when she was at her lowest point, but there was nothing real from spirit I could give her. The line was dead.

A few months passed and Jackie phoned me one weeknight evening in floods of tears. 'You know, Gordon, the kids have gone to bed and I'm sitting here on my own thinking about my mum and it's just so hard.'

I was trying to console her when I was suddenly aware of her father's presence.

'Jacks, you know who's here? Your dad's impressing something on my mind. He's telling me your mum's going to come through in a way that's so concrete it's better than any reading I could do for you.'

'You think so?'

'I know this time. And she won't need me to do it.'

That Saturday Jackie called me and she was like another woman – the energy bursting out of her was incredible.

'Gordon, you'll never believe what happened!'

'Tell me!'

'I was sitting here, just totally low and saying, "Mum, just give me a sign – anything." And the phone rang and I picked it up and I heard my mum's voice, absolutely her voice, and she said, "I'm OK, darling. I'm OK." And then the phone went dead and there was this horrible noise. I dialled 1471 and you know what? It was my mum's phone number. That house is empty, the line's been disconnected. How can that happen?'

'I don't know, but I think I know why your dad wouldn't come through to you before. He didn't have any good news for you and your mum because he knew she was going to die. He couldn't have told you that because you would have been so distressed – you'd have been crushed to know you only had a few weeks with her.'

We talked more and then Jackie rang off, still on a real high from her mother's message. I'd guess also that her mother hadn't sent a message via me because I knew the family too well and it wouldn't have been any great proof. Spirit not only has a window into the future but also the wisdom to know when to give a message and how much of the news to pass on and in what manner – the way that gives the most proof.

Predictions have to be productive for spirit to pass them on. Sometimes they'll alert us to a health problem. It's logical enough – if you've already begun to be sick, the timeline for that illness has begun. But the message is almost always positive, even if it doesn't seem so at first glance.

For reasons best known to spirit, Albert Best was especially gifted at producing messages which would sometimes take years to unravel but did predict the future. I remember him telling me that in the 1980s a distinguished-looking man approached him after a demonstration and said, 'Mr Best, thank you for helping me.' Albert had no idea who he was and the man explained.

In the late 1960s Albert had been working with a circle of mediums in Irvine that was extremely highly regarded and would get some incredible communications. One evening, one of the women in the circle was in a trance when a spirit guide came through and told them that there was a man out on a road in the Scottish countryside and that they had to go and find him because he would save many lives.

It was the dead of winter, but the mediums set out in the snow to the location they'd been given, wading through drifts up a narrow lane with no sign of life in it. But there, curled up in the snow, was a down-and-out with wild hair and weeks of unkempt beard growth. He was freezing to death.

They gathered him up, despite his protests that he didn't want any help, got him back on his feet and drove him back to Albert's place. They got him warm and put him to bed, realizing with a shock that he was actually quite a young man, but obviously one who was in despair. They didn't ask him any questions.

The next day he had revived a little but was still very obviously depressed. Coaxed for details as to why he'd been out in the snow, he told them that he was a doctor whose wife had died only a short time after they'd married and who'd been so grief-stricken that he'd wanted to leave his old life and die.

Albert brought some of the other mediums in his circle round and they sat to see if they could reach the man's wife. Albert was an incredible medium and, as I said, this circle in Irvine was exceptional, but I don't think even they were expecting what happened: the young man's wife appeared in physical form, right there in Albert's living room, in her wedding dress. She spoke to her husband directly, reassuring him that she was safe and happy and that he mustn't give up on himself.

It's no wonder that after that extraordinary experience the man's life changed. The distinguished-looking doctor who came to the demonstration to thank Albert 20 years later had moved to America and become a leading oncologist who had indeed, as the spirit guide had predicted, saved many lives.

Spirit doesn't need to communicate via a medium to intervene in the fates of people in this life. I gave a private reading in the spring of 2005 in London for a young Indian man I'll call Arun, who'd suffered the harrowing loss of two family members. He was very nervous and sceptical initially, demanding to know if I could read his thoughts, and when I told him I couldn't do that but that someone in spirit could pick up on what he was thinking and communicate with him via me, I don't think he believed me.

I left it up to his relatives in spirit to convince him, which they did, coming through in fine form with a sarcastic comment or two and making him laugh. I watched as this man gradually dropped his guard and showed how vulnerable he'd been left by a year of harrowing emotional events.

It had already been an incredibly healing reading, but then I got the sense of another spirit trying to reach this man. This time it was a young man. He said he had been shot just before his twenty-first birthday. The man sitting opposite nodded, his face showing surprise, as he'd lost this friend years ago.

The man in spirit then went on to say, 'Aren't you glad I saved your life at Christmas?'

The man was shocked. 'How do you know that?' he asked me. I promised him I had no idea what the spirit was referring to, I was only passing on a message. When the sitting was over, he explained what had happened.

Like the South African family, he'd been staying in Thailand for Christmas with his girlfriend and their four kids. On Christmas Eve he had got an overwhelming impulse to switch hotels, because the place they were staying in wasn't going to offer them much of a party over the holidays – both alcohol and dancing were banned there. I suppose that they could have stayed in the same place and just gone to a restaurant or club to celebrate, but he couldn't resist the restlessness, so they packed up their bags and moved.

The new hotel he chose was much further back from the sea and suited them well. On Boxing Day morning he'd booked a diving lesson for himself and the kids at 7 a.m., but he'd also booked a band to play on Christmas Day, so they'd celebrated in style, drinking and dancing till the early hours.

The next morning he'd opened his bleary eyes, gone to the window, pushed back the curtains and looked at his watch as he strapped it onto his wrist. It was 9 a.m.

– he'd missed the diving lessons. He was just cursing himself and thinking that he'd let down the kids when he focused on the scene outside the window.

His girlfriend came up to stand beside him and he turned to her and said, 'Where is everything?'

All they could see was water. The buildings were gone. His old hotel was gone. The trees and cars and people were gone.

They stared at each other in horror, barely able to understand what had transformed the scene below them. 'Oh God,' was the next reaction, 'where are the kids?' They raced to the kids' room but it was empty. They ran up and down the corridors, calling out to them, searching every place they thought they might be till they found them in the swimming pool on the rooftop, splashing away happily. The entire family had been completely unaware that the tsunami had struck.

The man told me that the first thing he'd done was to get his family out, but he didn't go with them, staying behind instead to help others. He went on to make a significant contribution to the rescue effort.

As we sat there in my living room, he said, 'You know, when I got that urge to move hotels, something in my heart told me it was out of the ordinary. It felt like divine inspiration, but I didn't really think about why until now, when you confirmed it for me.'

Intervention by someone in spirit represents part of a particular timeline too. If we miss one potential ending because of advice from spirit, then that advice came through because it was part of our destiny.

Spirit messages often come as a result of an incredible chain of synchronicity that draws a person to the communication. It's common for someone who's never thought of attending a Spiritualist church to find a series of coincidences drawing them to receive a particular message at a particular time.

A friend of mine was living with a man she loved but who had a bad temper which sometimes scared her. He'd begun to get increasingly possessive and obsessed by the idea that she might meet other men. One day an old friend of hers reappeared in her life and started raving about her visits to the Spiritualist church, where she said she'd got lots of messages. My friend was intrigued, so shortly afterwards she attended a service. Her boyfriend let her go to it because he thought there would be mainly women there and no men to steal her away.

At the church she sat quietly, listening as loved ones in spirit brought evidence through and their families in the audience smiled as they heard about how happy they were on the other side and how they still cared for them.

Then the medium on the platform singled her out, saying, 'That lady there, I have your mother here.'

As she'd recently lost her mother, my friend accepted it, expecting to have a message like the others she'd been hearing, but to her horror the medium went on, 'Your mother says you must leave your house. There's a gun there which you will find if you go and look for it and there's a bullet with your name on it.'

You can imagine the consternation this caused. My friend was dumbstruck. She got up a little shakily and drove home.

Once there, running on instinct, she walked straight to her partner's wardrobe and rummaged through some of his clothes. There was the gun her mother had warned her about. She put it back, packed some things and fled.

Could you ignore a message like that from spirit?

3

'Did I Have a Premonition?'

The other week the phone rang quite late one evening and I answered and found an anxious friend at the other end. He had a teenage son who was just off on a school trip to South Africa and he had got himself into a real state because he was convinced that the boy was going to be killed. 'I had a dream that he died,' he said. 'It must be a premonition. Tell me, is he going to be OK or should I stop him going?'

This was just days after another friend, a businessman, had phoned me from an airport on the other side of the world, out of breath with panic. 'I just got off a plane,' he said.

'Oh, where are you?' I asked, thinking he was on holiday somewhere exciting.

'I just got on it,' he went on, brushing aside my question, 'and I had this gut feeling that it would crash after take-off, so I walked off. I was right to do it, wasn't I? It must have meant something.'

When you have a sudden fear and a terrible image shoots into your mind, it's tempting to believe that it's a 'gut instinct' telling you not to do something, a premonition of some kind of disaster. I've certainly experienced several distinct episodes of second sight in my life when I'd be half-awake and see, for example, my brother having an accident which did occur the next day. I always know when one of these 'dreams' is a true premonition because they end in a kind of popping sound in my ears, as though I'm coming back to the here and now. Could the friends who phoned have been sensing echoes from the future too?

When someone tells me about a 'vision of the future' I have to look closely at what they think they're predicting and where they are now. In these cases it only took a moment to realize that these 'echoes' were coming from the men's pasts, not the future. The father with the teenage son had just lost both his parents within a month of each other, while the businessman had just squandered a tremendous amount of money and a chunk of his business. Their dreams and panics weren't so much premonitions as dread based on a terrible life occurrence that they were afraid would strike again. Their fear and loss had grown so huge that they were poisoning their thinking. They wanted reassurance from me about the future, but were overlooking something that was in them right now.

I told the businessman that I couldn't tell him to get back on the plane because obviously he would have a terrible flight and be a nervous wreck at the end of it. The plane took off without him and it didn't crash, but he had a hell of a job reorganizing his travel arrangements and was left fretting at the airport. As for the father, I tried to reassure him and just hoped that his fear didn't ruin things for his son on a trip of a lifetime. The boy did survive his time in South Africa just fine, in spite of his father's dream.

The trouble is that when you are mentally and emotionally in a place of great fear and darkness, every thought you have is distorted by that fear. The businessman could have been in first class having grapes peeled for him by a stewardess and the father could have been down the pub with friends, having some time off from ferrying his teenage son around and nagging him to do his homework, but both of them were bogged down in emotions and fears.

Even though I had some genuine psychic experiences and episodes of real precognition as a boy, I was also haunted by the terrible fear that my parents were going to die. I'm sure a lot of kids go through this. My mum would pop out to the shops and I'd picture her being run over by a car, my dad would be half an hour late coming home and I'd think he'd had a heart attack. As I started to get real precognitions I became more and more afraid of these 'visions' of my parents. If some of my visions came true, surely they all would sooner or later?

Well, my dad died peacefully in his hospital bed at 82 and my mum's still with us, so it just goes to show how wrong my 'premonitions' were. How much time did I spend going over horrible things which never happened? I didn't even stop when I grew up. As a young man I always assumed that I was going to die young, and I remember sitting over my son Paul when he was a baby and thinking, 'What's going to happen to him without a father? What if he dies? How could I bear that?' I think every parent goes through that, even the most zen.

It's a waste of energy, though, and, more importantly, a terrible frame of mind in which to make decisions. If my businessman friend couldn't even get on a plane without thinking everything was an omen, how could he have undertaken a risky new business venture with any judgement?

It's rare for people to tap into precognitive vision and when we experience it, it's not something we choose to do. Although I've had many predictive dreams or sudden impressions that something will happen to a friend, it's not as though I can switch it on and off when I need it.

The famous medium William Thomas Stead drew many spirit-inspired pictures of ocean liners sinking and wrote two accounts of imagined maritime disasters, one even involving a White Star Line ship, but he still boarded the *Titanic* in Southampton and went down with it.

If, like Stead, you're involved in the future event, a vision or sense of something ominous in the future could be coming from your own timeline and be something that will affect you directly, or it could just be something that will happen in your own lifetime and have a great mental imprint on you, for example if you're sitting in Glasgow and picturing the Twin Towers falling on the other side of the world. We may not even be aware of the force that pushes us away from or towards a certain situation, but it will always be something out of the ordinary.

I meet a lot of people who want me to tell them what's going to happen in their future so they can relax now and take comfort from it or else be prepared for the worst. Will their business be a success? Will they find a husband? Will their kids be OK? I understand that they just want to be spared a life of uncertainty, but I can't dish out that kind of information. It's rare for me to have what you call precognitive messages. Which is just as well, because if I got messages about everyone's future all the time I'd never have a second to do anything else.

There are many tried and trusted ways of trying to look along a timeline and predict the future – from reading tea leaves or palms to peering into crystal balls, watching birds' flight paths and shuffling tarot cards – but they have their limits. The result you get is all about where you are at the time of the reading, and nothing is set in stone. The reader might pick up the fact that in the future you will face a choice and if you pick one option you will end up meeting a particular person and if you pick the other you will meet someone else altogether. What that reader can't do is tell you about your entire life and every emotion you will have along those timelines. They can only pick up what state you're in as you sit opposite them and make a prediction based on that.

If you do use a system like the tarot on a regular basis, be very aware of your reasons for doing so. Lots of us are desperately seeking answers to the problems in our lives, but the first place to look to solve these problems is inside yourself, in identifying the nature of your fears and seeing what you can do to overcome them and live your life day by day. Any good tarot practitioner knows that the tarot contains lessons and thinking points, not answers. If you keep going back to the cards to ask for a definitive future, you're not letting anything unfold without this magical 'outside' influence.

There is one way, however, that I think we *can* get a snapshot of a timeline. When I was travelling around the UK on a book tour in the spring of 2009, someone in an audience in Edinburgh asked me a great question: 'Could *déjà vu* happen because your life has a blueprint and it's part of your destiny?'

I liked the idea that because everything was laid out somewhere in the ether for us, we could get glimpses of it from time to time. 'It could be,' I said. 'It makes good sense. It's not a past life but something from this life that you plotted to be there and here it is.'

Déjà vu tells you that there's some bigger force rolling along with you. The way it strikes you and penetrates your body and mind, making you feel as though you've been knocked out of the normal world for a second, tells me that it involves a connection with a higher part of your consciousness.

The funny thing was, on the next night of the book tour someone asked exactly the same question in exactly the same phrasing. And the same thing happened on the next date, and on the date after that. If that's not *déjà vu*, I don't know what is!

4

'Can We Know
When We Will Die?'

In 1994 the magazine *Psychic News* gave a Spiritualist of the Year award, to be presented at Lewisham Theatre. It was a full house of over a thousand people and when Albert Best's name was called out, there was a huge outbreak of applause in appreciation of his incredible work. What happened next stunned the audience into silence.

Albert went on stage to collect his award, and to his surprise and everyone else's horror, spontaneously gave a message.

'You over there, that lady. You live in Chelsea,' he said, pointing to an elderly lady in the audience and then giving her street and house number.

'Yes, I live there.'

'Your husband is here,' said Albert and gave the man's name.

'That's him,' she nodded.

'You'll be joining him,' said Albert and then in front of the appalled audience he gave the date and time of her death.

You could have heard a pin drop. It was scandalous – mediums are not supposed to share predictions like that. How dare this brilliant medium overstep the mark? What was he thinking?

Everyone was wondering what kind of hell that poor woman would go through when she piped up, 'Thank you, Mr Best. I've been waiting to hear that.' And she didn't seem in the least bothered.

In their next issue, *Psychic News* ran a headline about this 'atrocious' prediction, but a week later they printed a retraction. The woman had in fact died precisely when Albert had predicted and her family told *Psychic News* that she'd been very happy to have the warning, as she had been ready to go and wanted it to be sooner rather than later.

I asked Albert how on earth he did it and he shrugged. 'Gordon, it was spontaneous. All predictions are. You can't make them up, you can't stop them when they come, you can't influence them. If anyone else in that audience had asked me when they were going to die, I couldn't have told them.'

Some exceptional people do know pretty much when they are going to pass into spirit. My Auntie Sylvia could assess how long she had left when she was dying of stomach cancer because of the years she had spent as a Macmillan nurse, watching the sick move through those final stages.

Very early on, when I hadn't learned what a terrible question it was to put to someone, I asked Mrs Primrose if she knew how she would die, and although she frowned, she said, 'Actually, son, I do.'

'How can you know that and who told you?'

She answered very simply, 'Spirit has shown me that I'll be in my chair and I'll fall asleep and then just walk out of my body.'

About two years later that's exactly what she did. Her home help found her sitting in her chair with a smile on her face and a heap of Christmas presents all bought, wrapped and labelled.

My friend Dronma's name was once sent to a Tibetan Buddhist astrologer, who sent her a detailed chart of her life, despite having nothing but her name to go by. There was no single line of destiny, more a tree of branches: if she took this option, her life would go this way, if she took another, that way. This included not one exit date but three – the first when she was in her early fifties and had had major surgery. She did have surgery then and it saved her life, but she thinks the doctors were able to do that because she still had something to do: to meet a high lama and present him with a *thangka*, a devotional painting, that she had completed. Her next turn off the motorway (as it were) is at 66, which she thinks is pretty reasonable.

What would you do if you had such an insight? It's a terrifying thought and the only way to turn it into an advantage is to use the time to prepare yourself and your loved ones, to live up to that last moment and to aim higher in the next world.

I'll always remember a redoubtable lady I knew at the Spiritualist church in Glasgow called Effie Ritchie, who was one of those huge souls who only seem to get more generous the more they give of themselves. Towards the end of her life, when she was very sick, she went through a phase where she would get scared and call me up for a conversation. Finally, she said, 'Right, I've got to go and have another chat with God and sort this out,' and the next day she rang sounding like her old self. God had obviously cleared up a thing or two for her and she wanted me to do her hair so that she looked presentable when she met Him.

She was at home in her living room, not the hospital, in the last few days and she had all her sons and grandchildren gathered round her and created a real atmosphere of normality for them, not only to make it easier for them but also because she was living bang up to her last breath. I remember her splitting her sides with laughter when the insurance salesman came round and tried to talk her into extending her policy – 'Those guys are really something, aren't they?' she gasped – and she renewed it for a week and no more.

Right to the end she held the centre, and what a gesture of love that was: she'd brought her sons into the world and taught them how to live in it, and now she was teaching them how to leave it.

5

'Can I Change my Destiny?'

When I started going to mediumship classes and meditating, I began to realize just how much of life and what you might call destiny was beyond my control. Some timelines are obvious – book a holiday in France and you'll probably end up going on holiday in France – but sometimes you have no idea when you've begun a course of events that will lead you to something personally devastating. It's as though you're on an escalator which carries you to an inevitable conclusion.

One of the hardest things is recognizing what you can change and what you can't. Sometimes we think we've got it all sorted and that everything will run according to a plan we've decided on and then suddenly it all breaks down.

I knew a woman called Heidi who started going out with a nice good-looking young man called Daniel. Right from the beginning she had very definite ideas about what their future would be like. After a particular length of time they'd get engaged, then married, and their first house would be in such and such a street, with a spare bedroom, but when she got pregnant, at a certain age, they would move to a bigger house ... and so on. She seemed to have everything planned for the next five years, including which Christmases they'd spend with her folks and which with her in-laws. And we'd say, 'Heidi, you've only been out for drinks with him,' but she did get him, and everything else. They got married, had the baby and bought the big house and we were all really impressed, but then she lost the child. We were all gutted for her. It wasn't some kind of punishment for daring to be happy, though, it was just one of those things that happens.

You can plan your life a little and have aims – say, you want to have a certain job when you're 30, or you'd rather have kids before you were 40 – but if you actually see yourself in precisely one place at precisely one date doing precisely one thing, then you're leaving out what might be the most important parts of your life. Why erase a whole realm of possibilities because you're focused on getting yourself five years down the road with a Labrador, a two-garage house and 2.4 children? You may get there but have missed out on life experiences that you badly needed. What if, say, you reached your goal of being rich and successful, then looked back on those years of work and realized you'd ignored your kids and what was happening in their lives and now they were strangers to you? What amazing, uplifting memories would you have lost in the meantime? That's when some people wake up and have a crisis.

Life is all about change. It's all about choice and it's all about bigger forces underlying those choices. The moment you realize that you are not meant to hold back that flow or try to divert it is a very liberating moment. You gain a kind of relaxation of the mind which makes it easier to handle the next thing that's thrown up.

You can reach a level where you can be spontaneous in a positive sense which isn't childish or reckless. It's not about having a rigid plan but acknowledging that you'll have to deal with constant change. With this type of spontaneity, you move towards a decision that has to be made rather than sitting down and labouring over the pros and cons. It just comes and you find yourself going there. That's the moment when you're going with life. And that's why trying to point people to their destiny is just trying to point them to the here and now.

To me, that ease comes from within. It's a deeper part of yourself. And you can only go with the flow like that when you're in control of your emotions — by which of course I don't mean repressing them, just that you don't let them dissect your plans. Otherwise you're lost in hypotheticals: 'What if I do that and this happens?' That's taking fear into your body and letting it influence your inner self. You can't stop the universe or control which timelines you end up on, but you can stop yourself making the most of your life out of sheer fear.

Bad things will come, true, but there are also a lot of highs and intense living and opportunities on our path if we relax enough to meet them and enjoy them when they do come. Stay interested, not afraid. Remember there are many, many timelines running through your life and not all of them end in sorrow.

Last time I was in South Africa I got chatting to the cab driver taking me across Soweto to my next appointment. We rolled down a road lined with people crouched in the dust, selling food and clothes. I knew where these people lived. You couldn't call it 'good living conditions' or even 'living conditions' – tiny corrugated metal huts crammed with whole families baking in the heat, dust and flies everywhere and barely any footholds to let you climb out and escape the shanty towns.

I had heard of some horrific crimes being committed there, but when I saw the place with my own eyes I could understand how hard it was for people to function or think in any normal kind of fashion. You could scrape a living by selling what you could get your hands on, or you could try and grow something (but how, in those packed dusty lanes?), or you could steal – and stealing usually meant violence. One man told me that life in prison was better than life in the townships. I could believe him.

As we were driving down the street, the taxi driver was silent for a moment, then he said, 'I see myself standing by the road with these people every time I pass.'

'Did you come from here?' I asked.

'Yes, I'm from this street,' he said. 'I started out selling things by the roadside too.'

I asked him how he'd got out and he said that his wife had made clothes that he had sold on the street, but he had had a bit more ambition than that. She was such a good tailor that he had started to take her work to the white shops, and the people there had liked what they saw and bought more of the clothes. His daughter was a talented seamstress too, so he had invested in a small shed and some sewing machines and the three of them had gone into business. Soon he no longer had to go to the roadside to sell the clothes and was able to buy a Mercedes and go out to work as a taxi driver. Soon he and his family were employing more people and had bought their own house and his son had gone abroad to university.

'Every time I pass these people I thank God for what I have,' he added, but I couldn't help thinking that this was nothing to do with God. He and his family had pulled themselves up out of the dust by sheer attitude and determination.

That man taught me that there's a way out of every situation, and it has nothing to do with cosmic ordering or offering up prayers for anything other than strength. He looked for it and he grabbed it. He is an example to us all: even a flower can grow in concrete.

I think that good fortune can also come from a state of mind and from good decisions. If you're open and positive, it's more likely that good opportunities will come your way and you'll be prepared to grasp them when they do, which is exactly what this man had done. It can take a long journey of harsh experiences before you reach the point where you can do that, but it is always worth it.

When I'd popped outside for a quick smoke after a demonstration in London one day I met a young woman who'd been in the audience, and who, though she hadn't had anything to ask, had clearly been paying lots of attention to everyone there, not just me.

'You know,' she said, 'when that woman stood up and asked, "Why do people constantly do bad things?" I thought to myself, "My God, that woman is angry. And that's what's holding her back."'

I was intrigued by this reaction and asked her where she was coming from, so she told me her story.

As a teenager she'd been a bright girl from a loving family, but she'd got involved with a bad crowd and one day she'd been attacked and raped by one of the boys in the gang. She'd had no support from the police or from other people she'd told, who were scared of the boy, so he was never prosecuted.

After that she began to hate the world, furious that he'd got away with his crime. She really went off the rails. She fell in with an even dodgier group of people and started going out with a drug dealer. She was taking drugs herself by now and rowing with her family and friends, creating a lot of pain. She began selling stuff for her boyfriend and he planned that she should go out on the game for him, and because in her anger she had just about no self-worth, she didn't have a problem with that.

In the end she was arrested for drug dealing before that could happen and served a nine-month sentence. She was locked up alongside many women who had committed horrendous crimes and she truly thought that this was the level on which she belonged. She didn't think she'd amount to anything more and wished she just didn't exist at all.

When she got out it was as though the whole world agreed with her. She had some good qualifications, but she applied for a string of jobs and was turned down every time. She didn't think there could be any reason other than she was cursed – why should she have to go through this and not the boy who'd raped her years ago?

Finally, in yet another interview, she cracked. She sat down opposite the owner of the company and let rip. 'I might as well tell you why there's a gap in my CV,' she began, and she told him the whole story, from the rape to the drug dealing to her time in prison, while he just struggled to contain his shock. It was actually the first time she'd told anyone everything and she said it must have changed her entire demeanour – even if you're not actively lying, when you try to hide something so big you'll inevitably end up looking shifty.

And the most magical thing was that when she'd finished, the man cleared his throat, shuffled her CV and said, 'You need a chance and I'm going to offer you one.' He gave her the job.

And that was the point when her 'bad luck' changed and her life started to improve. Like a lot of people who go through something terrible, she'd reacted to it by making life worse for herself and those around her. She'd been so angry that no one could get close to her, but now she found that her mother was supportive and she was able to rebuild herself.

The attack had left her terrified and that fear had turned to anger, which had been as effective as a curse on her life, but it was a curse that, as it turned out, she was able to lift herself.

The karma or luck she was working with was just like everybody else's – it was created by her actions, by what she chose to do at a given moment, because of how she felt. Initially she was unable to move on from what had happened. She felt worthless and angry and her life spiralled out of control, but when she was honest about who she was and how she'd ended up there, she saw a light in the darkness and others recognized it in her.

If you create an atmosphere of bad luck around yourself, you will stop evolving and there will probably be consequences, some of which are obvious and straightforward.

I had a hairdressing client who got into a car when he was drunk and hit a child, who was gravely injured. He lost his licence and, as his job had depended on his ability to drive, he lost his income too. The thing was, he put all this down to bad luck. He genuinely thought that as this was the first time he'd driven under the influence, it was some kind of terrible coincidence that a child had happened to get injured. But the whole process was a timeline that he had begun by deciding against his better instincts to drive when he was over the limit. Yes, there was a chance that he might have got home safely, but he was the one who introduced the possibility that someone would be hurt. And his inability to take responsibility for this kept him unconscious of his own choices in life.

Whatever our circumstances, we all have some room for manoeuvre and choice. The realization of this often comes in the wake of one of those life-defining moments that's beyond our control. One of my friends in Glasgow, Christine Peebles, became a brilliant example of how to understand fate. I've told some of her story in earlier books, because it altered the course of my own life.

She worked in the hairdresser's with me and lost one of her brothers, Brian, in a fire, and it was when she was grieving for him that we first went to a Spiritualist church, where she had a message from the medium, Mary Duffy. What I've never described is the way that Christine came through that dark time and how she did something incredible with it. Her story is a remarkable example to me of what can be achieved in even the most difficult of circumstances.

Christine might have been forgiven for thinking that she was doomed to have a terrible life – whether you believe in family curses or bad backgrounds or people who 'come to no good' or not, she didn't have the best start. Her mother died in tragic circumstances when she was very young, leaving her and her brothers alone when they were barely adults. After her death, Brian and Christine left the old family home, banded together and decided to share a flat. In order to get a bigger one, they rented a room to a guy called John, who was a friend of Brian's. Brian chose a place on the top floor of the house. He nearly managed to set it on fire one night when he came in, started cooking some eggs and fell asleep. Then, one night six weeks after they'd moved in, Christine woke up to find flames dancing under her bedroom door and the fire brigade bursting into the flat. She tried to go to the living room to find Brian but couldn't see him anywhere. John stopped her running into the flames. Brian never made it out.

Brian had been Christine's big brother, the easy-going, good-looking guy who was almost all the family she had. She went through every stage of grief – the horror, the misery and the anger at herself and Brian. 'You have no idea,' she told me, 'of the number of nights I spent beating myself up, saying, "You idiot, why didn't you save him?"' She was furious with him, too, for really setting the place on fire that time.

Our salon was in one of the roughest parts of Glasgow and we had plenty of junkies and alcoholics coming in, and we'd try to help, but Christine at first found it hard not to grit her teeth because she felt they were wasting their lives when her brother had lost his. John was the only person who could understand what she'd been through and they eventually married and had a little girl.

Five or six years after the fire I had the first message from Brian. When I was on holiday in America I dreamed of him showing me what had happened. He'd come home from work, had a drink, lit a cigarette and dozed off on the couch. The cigarette had fallen onto the floor and the carpet had caught light. Brian had woken up and rushed into the little recess kitchen they'd had. He'd tried to use wet towels to put the fire out, but there were bars on the windows and he had been trapped. He put a towel over his head and before the firemen could reach him he had suffocated. His body hadn't even been burnt. Christine had said she didn't want to know exactly what had happened to him, so I kept quiet about the dream.

At that time we used to go to a meditation class together and one night when I was sitting chatting to her afterwards she asked me why I'd never had a message for her from Brian. Then I had to admit that I had had something from him. 'He's OK,' I said, and left it at that, but she wasn't going to be put off: 'There's more to it than that, isn't there?' Finally I told her the whole story.

A few weeks later a friend of hers who was a youth club worker attended a talk given by the local fire brigade and got chatting to one of the firemen. She asked him which district he worked in, and when he said, 'West End, Glasgow,' she said, 'Oh my God, my friend's brother died in a fire there.' The fireman asked if it was Buckingham Terrace and she nodded. Then he told her how they had found Brian and everything I'd told Christine tallied.

When Christine got this second confirmation she was able to say that she actually felt better about having the knowledge – Brian had obviously wanted her to know as proof that he was still with her. For the first time she felt that he was trying to help her come to terms with what had happened.

Slowly she began to stop feeling 'like a zombie' and came back to the land of the living. She started to wake up and develop herself spiritually and stop being so angry. She told me, 'Brian wasn't taken from me, he died. By his own hand, really. He didn't deserve it, it just happened.' She realized there was no point being angry at him for it or shaking her fist at God. And although her marriage to

John didn't last, she knew that she'd never have had that relationship or her daughter if Brian hadn't passed.

After a while she also started to think about ways in which she could make a difference. She quit hairdressing, found a little job in a social work department and took every opportunity that came her way to train. She was offered the chance to do a degree and she seized it, and soon she found herself going round houses as a full-time social worker.

'I thought I'd lived,' she told me, 'but then I saw the levels of abuse that children suffer, experience and survive. And I had to make decisions that shaped people's lives.'

She thought about losing her own mother and realized that she could have had a very different life. She had grown up surrounded by other people's bad karma, but had refused to make it her own.

'The number of times I put it down to bad luck and cursed,' she said, 'and that's what I needed to tell myself at the time. But there are people who tell themselves that and then they adopt everything that's bad as an extension of the "curse". I didn't want to do that. I knew I had a right to be happy.'

She broke free and now she has to use that same judgement to do her job well.

'When crap happens,' she told me, 'I just stand above the situation and say, "Is that mine? No. I will not take it on or own it, it's not mine," and then I roll up my sleeves and get on with things.'

With her job she's right in the thick of some of the saddest, darkest ways of life, a constant reminder of what could have happened to her, but she can rationalize it and she can sleep at night. For all her spiritual practice, she's very down to earth.

Watching her over the years, it's incredible how whole she's become as a person. She hasn't forgotten the tragedies, just accepted them and that they weren't her fault. I've always thought she was amazingly courageous, even though she can be quite girly and fragile, but I don't think she realized it herself when she was younger. Time did resolve her grief, but she also needed to get up and do things and go out to work, and she did. She knew the value of being in the thick of life and not trying to leave it behind. She's a credit to people who've had loss.

She once asked me what our lives would have been like if Brian hadn't died. I know I would have been a hairdresser with a perm and a moustache, but who knows what would have happened to Christine? What I do know is that she took control of her karma and recognized that even a timeline where you suffer a great loss is not the only timeline you're on. In her life there was a timeline that ended in Brian's death and one that began with the fire and led her to help people who were desperately in need. The twist of fate that meant that she lived while Brian died ended up giving her an impressive clarity and gave every new day a value it hadn't had before. She was able to grasp some of the big truths in life and make a difference to others. You could say that she was 'saved for a purpose' – but that's how *she* made it work out.

The trick is to work with what you can. Some destinies we can't change, but life still gives us many chances. We can't dodge the bullet, pull our loved ones from the flames or cancel the plane journey that ends in a crash unless our lives were meant to work out that way, but we all have the opportunity to do something, improve our awareness and help others.

If we have a near miss ourselves, we can let it open our mind. Don't become fatalistic – you're not here to become resigned to whatever life throws at you, or to be paralysed with fear or do nothing, you're here to try to progress emotionally, mentally and spiritually. These are the reasons we are all here.

Ultimately, there is no other place to walk into except destiny – wherever you arrive is where you were meant to be. You can't cheat it – you'll only end up where you were always going to be.

6

'Is There a Soul Mate Out There for Me?'

Even if people want to escape destiny in some respects, there's one area where they're more than happy to think that fate will set them on the right timeline. I've lost count of the number of times that people have asked me about their love lives. Are they on the right path? Is a future mate part of their life plan? If they've been through some bad experiences, does that mean they should remain alone?

Some of the biggest highs and lows we experience in this world come from our romantic lives. It's one area of life where we're primed to share very deep parts of ourselves and to expect that that care and affection will be reciprocated. It can also be full of uncertainty, and people want reassurance that they'll find that perfect partner.

One night in the 1980s my brother Tommy was out late, walking down Tolcross Road in the east end of Glasgow. He saw something glinting by the kerb and bent down to see what it was. He picked up a woman's engagement ring – a solitaire diamond. There wasn't a soul in the street and because he didn't know what to do with the ring he took it home, stuck it in a drawer and forgot about it.

Twenty years later he was out of work and out of his marriage. One night he got talking with the barmaid in his local and they hit it off. They started to see one another and when they were out on a date Tommy told her about his marriage and she chimed in and said, 'Oh, I was engaged once, but I broke it off. We had a big row in the street and I pulled off my ring and threw it away.'

A bell rang in Tommy's head and he suddenly remembered that diamond solitaire. 'Where did you have that argument? When was it?' he asked her.

She said, 'Oh, Tolcross Road,' and told him when it happened.

'You're not going to believe this,' said Tommy, and she *didn't* believe it till he dug the ring out and showed it to her, and of course it was the same diamond she'd chucked in the gutter all those years ago. She and Tommy are married now. Was that a coincidence or a small sign that, once they were together, gave them a little piece of proof that they'd been on track to find each other?

I think it's when we're thinking about our love lives that we are happiest bandying words like 'fate' and 'destiny' around – we grow to believe that what we have with someone is so special that something from a higher, brighter level of consciousness must be involved in bringing us together. It's true that when two people come together there can be a powerful chain of synchronicities along the way and it's in our relationships that we come closest to having an understanding of a higher collective spirit that joins all of us together. A truly great relationship, we think, transforms us into better people all round. We also like to talk about soul mates – being two halves of the same heart – and to think that there is one special relationship out there for us that will move us profoundly.

So, if we are single and want a love that will be life-changing, surely that special individual will be delivered up to us by fate rather than internet dating? But the signs that point to a future with someone are often small – they don't come with a fanfare and they only provide confirmation much later. Tommy and his wife, for example, were on a path in life that didn't lead them straight to one another. If he had met her the night she threw the ring away, they probably wouldn't have had the same relationship that they had 20 years later, when they were older and wiser. Life doesn't always work out like the plot in a romantic novel, although the twists and turns will deliver us to the right person at the right time.

A friend of a friend was in her late twenties and becoming very depressed about being single. One winter she was out driving when her car skidded on ice and ran into a tree. The engine was rammed back against her legs by the force of the impact and though she wasn't badly injured, she was trapped and unable to move. The emergency services arrived and several firemen set to work painstakingly cutting her out of the wreckage. One of them stayed by her side and held her hand. It took an hour to get her free. When you are terrified, time often stretches into infinity, so you can imagine how long it felt for her, and there was this man holding her hand throughout the whole traumatic experience and talking to her gently. She felt that when he took her hand something special had passed between them.

When she had recovered a few weeks later she was still thinking of him and decided to get in touch. They saw each other a couple of times and soon it blossomed into a relationship. She thought that she was in love and what could be more perfect? She hadn't just been in a wrecked car, she'd been in a wrecked life, and he had been the hero who had come and rescued her. Surely it was all predestined. Why else would he have been working that night?

A couple of years later they moved to the other side of Glasgow and set up home together. The trouble was, she didn't get to see much of her hero because he was always out working long hours, rescuing other people. I think she fell in love with the hero rather than the man, but of course a long relationship needs more than repeating the single act of saving someone over and over again.

She ended up signing up to an evening class in counselling at a local college to fill in the hours when he couldn't be with her. As part of the class, the students had to pair up and practise counselling techniques and dialogues on one another, and she worked with a man called Adam. Maybe you're ahead of me and can guess what happened – Adam was the man she had the true connection to, a connection which went far deeper than the rescue. Eventually she split from the fireman and married Adam, and they now have two kids and are still very much in love. That car crash did set her on a track to meet the love of her life, but she had to learn some lessons about the real nature of love on the way. There was nothing so dramatic about the way she found Adam, but what they shared was stronger and more profound.

Sometimes when people think they're crazily in love, the 'love' is bigger than anything – bigger than the real person that they're reaching out to. An underlying problem is overwhelming their emotions and instead of being truly open and clear-eyed, they usually end up doing the wrong thing and it ends in disaster.

This often results in unrequited love and that's one of the hardest lessons for us to deal with. How can we have such strong feelings and get nothing in return?

When I was working with the Spiritualist church in England in the late 1990s a lady called Helen joined the group. She was in her late forties and had had the worst kind of life, with a bunch of men who were no good and lots of kids she'd had to bring up on her own. She obviously had a great need for support and affection, and though she never got particularly strong messages from the other side, she did get a lot of love from people in this plane for the first time – everyone in the church looked out for her and asked how she was. She loved to hug everyone and tell them, 'Now you remember this, I love you,' and though she was obviously on the path to learning something, it quickly became clear that she didn't have a clue what real love was.

The trouble was that she got fixated on a guy in the group who had his own complex – he thought he was Jesus, or at least that he was as important as Him. He was married, with a family, and not at all interested in Helen as a lover – he saw her as a follower and a friend. That's how she painted herself too. It was, she insisted, purely a soul partnership. They had been 'Red Indians' together hundreds of years ago – he had been the chief and she had been his squaw. She'd tell him she loved him and he was a brother to her, but then they'd row because the tension was too high, inevitably, and then she'd cuddle him and say that it was all OK. As Jesus, he clearly wasn't going to see the relationship as sexual, and although she viciously denied it, you could tell that whenever she'd had affection from men in her life it had been sexual and that was what she was seeking now. It was so plain that even her daughters were telling her she was making a fool of herself.

One woman in the church who'd become friendly with her tried to have a quiet chat with her, and say, 'Look, darling, you've just fallen in love with this man and you need to see it for what it is. But he's not going to be your partner and live the rest of his life with you. He's married and got kids.'

Helen was furious: 'How dare you say it's sex?' Then she stormed off and added another bit to her fantasy. She thought her friend had also been a squaw – a squaw who'd stabbed her through the heart to get her Red Indian chief!

By this stage she was buying oils and going to Jesus's house to wash his feet like Mary Magdalene, and his wife had had enough. His marriage was under threat and finally he had to break the news to Helen that nothing sexual was ever going to happen between them.

Of course, she was outraged once more: 'That was never on my mind – how dare you put that to me?' And then it must have dawned on her that it was obvious to everyone, although she was in deep denial. So she turned on us all and we were all 'evil' and 'possessed by bad spirits' and she took off into her own fantasy life and never came back to the church.

We tried to help and ground her, but she was having none of it. I know she had a breakdown a short time later and for a while she turned against everything religious and spiritual. Last time I passed her in the street I asked her how she was and she walked by briskly, saying, 'I'm not supposed to talk to people like you.' Recently I heard she was joining a Hindu community because she thought one of the teachers was connected to her in a previous life!

She went so far to avoid the here and now that she turned away from people who could have helped her. It would have been painful to have faced the fact that this man didn't desire her, but rather than admit it she built whole worlds of elaborate denials. Poor Jesus just wanted to be her friend, not run around with her for all eternity in a feather headdress!

You'd be amazed at the number of 'soul mates' like Helen and Jesus that I've met who have had difficult relationships or have fallen out and aren't even speaking to one another. So what is a soul mate? So many people want to think that they have a special connection to a person which already existed in spirit and has been destined to be fulfilled for hundreds of years and will survive death. They believe that their souls were just waiting in spirit to have a chance to connect on Earth this time round.

But why can't you just love somebody – as a great friend or a lover? Isn't this life big enough for you? Do you think you have to have a certain person for ever and ever?

It's a funny term to impose on two people, this soul thing. And the fact is we're *all* soul mates, we *all* connect on a higher level. We may be a part of each other's journey for a while, that's all.

I think real friendship and love involve not just that clear-eyed perspective but also an understanding of freedom and individuality rather than being a tie that binds two souls so closely that they're indistinguishable. You came together in the first place because you brought each other a fresh perspective, not so that you could become obsessed with each another to the exclusion of everything else. You don't own half of a person in a relationship, you've just met someone who resonates on the same level as you, so don't slap a label on it and expect them to behave a certain way.

It can be true, though, that an echo from a past life will draw us to someone in this one. On meeting them you may feel something that seems somehow much older and more rooted in you. The love you feel will be a recognition of that earlier life, but that doesn't mean that every single one of your lives is a tango with that one character and that you're twinned with them forever.

If I were to call any people in my life soul mates, it'd be Sandra and Christine, who are friends I've known since I was a teenager in Glasgow. But we don't live in one another's pockets. They came to stay recently and we had two days of the highest energy in my house and it was amazing. Then they went back home. Maybe I'll hear from one of them in a week or two with a text about some family news like a new grandchild, and then I'll give them a call and we'll catch up. I don't sit around creating a drama about the friendships, going, 'She needs me! I must be there! No one else will do,' but we know we'd be there for each other if we needed help.

Enjoy your soul mates and great loves, but don't let them shut you off from the world, because there will be other people out there who might also have that connection with you, and you should let them in too. Don't feel that because you have a relationship with one person you don't have to make the effort with other people any more. Who knows who's around the corner?

I don't totally dismiss the idea of a particularly strong predestined connection between two people, though, because I've seen it happen in real life.

I think one of the most amazing examples I've seen of a couple who had a connection from a past life was that of a lady called Stella and her husband Michael. At the time I learned their story I was doing a lot of healing work and a friend of mine called Carla Kinsella told me

I should meet them because Stella was a crystal healer. They lived in the countryside up in southern Scotland and Carla drove me out there one day.

They were a lovely couple, both in their forties, with four kids. When I asked if the two kids I was introduced to were twins, they laughed and explained. They'd both had two children in previous marriages and their older kids were the same age and so were the younger. Michael, who was an astrologer, had lost his wife to illness, and Stella's husband had been killed on duty as a soldier.

Both had become interested in past lives long before they met because they'd separately had recurring dreams that seemed to point to a story. In this life Stella was an army wife, moving around bases in Germany with her husband and children, but she had dreams about another time, one of the big Russian wars. In these she was always a young married woman waiting for her husband to come back from the front. Michael was also in the army, funnily enough being posted to the same bases as Stella but at slightly different times, so they never met. He also dreamed about a war in Russia, but he was a soldier who was killed so never went home, although he knew he had a wife waiting there for him.

Years after they'd both lost their spouses, they met at a mind, body, spirit festival and the recognition was mutual. Stella described it as instantly feeling comfortable and at home. As they talked, the coincidences began to pile up. Not only had they both been part of army families and lived on the same bases, they'd also been born the same year and as children had both been extremely ill at the same age. I doubt it was a surprise to either of them when they talked about their past-life experiences – Michael was clearly the young soldier husband that Stella had been waiting for.

Anything that comes into the here and now from a past life is there to be corrected, so that you can learn from it, accept it and move on. Think of healing and closure, not necessarily a new beginning. I think that's what impressed me most about Michael and Stella – once they had acknowledged that old connection, they barely referred to it again. It had all been resolved by them meeting and there was no need for them to talk about it constantly or try to go into trances and dig it all up again in order to prove how deeply they cared for each other. All that mattered was that they had come together – the shared past life was just a deep endorsement of that relationship.

Often in cases where a past life is making its presence felt, there's a great fear which needs to be overcome. It may be that in that life you died before you recognized something and now you have to finish that issue and grow. It may be that your spirit was preparing to come back into life at a higher level and then dashed back onto this plane to fix an emotional wound.

In this life you'll be drawn to a certain situation, perhaps a type of relationship, to enable you to do this.

It may be that previously you walked out on a family and this time you decide to stay or, like Stella and Michael, you went through the agony of separation and vowed to be reunited. Whatever it is, you have to live out that experience and burn up the bad karma, because it's made your spirit heavy. By facing it and learning, you gain understanding and your soul is lighter. Living something will help you understand it better than a lifetime of dwelling on the fear of it.

7

'Am I Unlucky in Love?'

If we can be fated to be with the right people, might it also be true that we can be fated to be with the wrong people? It can seem that way. Some people are stuck in a relationship Groundhog Day: over and over again they announce they've found someone new, but their friends and family realize, all too soon, that that someone just happens to have a few things in common with their ex. The relationship runs almost to a pattern and then it's all over and they're on their own again, wondering what went wrong. I've had people tell me they were 'destined' to repeat a mistake, which might sound like nonsense, but it's actually both right and wrong.

Some friends sent an older man called Dave to me for a reading, as he had become suicidal and they were terrified that, having failed once, he would try and take his life again. He had fallen head over heels for a guy who happened to be straight, but had convinced himself that he could turn his infatuation into a platonic friendship and help the younger man in life, as he was struggling a bit. He let him move into his home, gave him a bit of cash and they even went on a holiday or two together.

Of course, all Dave's friends could see that this situation was ridiculous. They'd seen him fall in love with unobtainable people before, although now he was taking it to a whole new level. But he assured them that it was all fine – he and the young man would just live together and be friends and that was that. He blinded himself to his real feelings and to the difficult situation he was creating.

After about ten months he went away on business and left the younger man in charge of the house. He returned a week later to find it stripped bare: the other man had systematically robbed him, even spitefully taking irreplaceable family photos and heirlooms that had only sentimental value. He'd obviously hated the growing tension in the house and had been biding his time, waiting to humiliate his 'friend'.

It needn't have taken that burglary for Dave to wake up and look at the cycle he was creating and the underlying reasons why he felt 'driven' to do it. Perhaps he didn't think he was worthy of a proper relationship and that's why he kept falling for people he could never have – if he'd found someone who truly loved him, he'd have had to see himself as deserving of that love. As it was, he let 'love' drag him into a nervous breakdown.

A relationship has no chance of success unless you go into it with clear eyes or grow to understand what drove you to it in the first place. I think of a beautiful woman I know who's in her fifties and thought she was constantly attracted to the wrong kind of men. After great beginnings, her relationships all seemed to sour and she would end up on her own once more, wondering what had happened.

She was chatting with me over a drink once about her 'terrible taste in men' when she suddenly changed her tone and said, 'You know, Gordon, the love of my life died when I was only in my early twenties.' I hadn't heard this part of her story, so I asked her about him.

They had met and fallen head over heels in love, although not everyone around them had shared their happiness. He was black and she was white, and friends and family of both of them were opposed to the match out of pure racism. One of her friends even said to her, 'It'll all end in tears,' but they defied everyone and married quickly, determined to stay together despite the hatred.

They were only in the early months of their marriage and still feeling as if they were on their honeymoon when he was killed in a car crash. She was devastated, but to her horror, her family acted as though his death was the best thing that could have happened. His family had no sympathy for her either, almost blaming her for the crash. We all feel alone in grief, but her isolation was doubled.

'Maybe he was the only person for me,' she suggested. 'I had my chance and found him and lost him, and that's it. You don't see anyone in my future, do you?'

I had to tell her that of course I did – *she* was the person she needed to find. She'd been a young woman in love and under pressure. Love is an altered state of consciousness and the beginning of any big relationship is enough to put you on another planet altogether, but eventually that bubble will pop and hopefully you'll be grounded and clear-sighted enough to get on with the real business of loving a real person rather than just falling in love with an incredible being. She hadn't had a chance in that marriage to get beyond the 'bubble' of falling deeply in love and in a way she'd been stuck there in a potent combination of grief and the most unreal, elevated love. When she was tragically bereaved, she'd been surrounded by people whose response was so cruel that she was left to deal with the raw grief alone. It was no wonder all her later relationships had fallen into bitterness – those men weren't necessarily 'bad', they'd just loved someone who could not love them back because she was still caught up with her lost husband. They cheated on her or became aggressive and frustrated because they sensed – even if she didn't – that they couldn't lift her out of that grief and make her love them. That was her job, not theirs. She needed to get back in touch with the woman who *could* have space for someone else in her heart of hearts.

Since we had that conversation she's taken a good six months to be on her own to heal and has now begun dating, though she's taking it very slowly, and for the first time since her marriage it's working out for her.

Many people go through bad relationships because they refuse to wake up and be honest with themselves – it's one thing to lie to a partner, but that deception begins with the lie you tell to yourself. My friend thought she just needed the right man to fix her and blamed them when it went wrong. Dave created a whole web of complications and bad emotions because he thought he could turn a situation to his advantage. They both let a pattern of behaviour taint their love lives.

Many people know they're with the wrong person but will use the word 'love' as a reason to stay when they haven't even really considered the meaning of it. One couple I knew, though, were able to look at the wreckage fearlessly, see their weaknesses and emerge stronger.

When I was working as a hairdresser I had a colleague called Anne who seemed to have quite a dramatic romantic life. She was only in her teens when she got into a serious relationship with a guy whom she loved but who had two bad habits, drinking and gambling. Not only was he hard on her, but he also spent all her cash, and her new hair salon, which she'd scrimped and saved to open, had to be sold to pay his debts.

She parted company with him and a few years later met a lovely guy called John, whom we all liked. They got married and had a couple of kids, and their professional life seemed to blossom too. Soon they had two salons of their own and they'd bought a big house, mortgaged up to the hilt.

All seemed well for years, but then John's moods began to deteriorate and it became obvious that he was turning into an alcoholic. He would drink and come home bruising for a fight, ready to swing a fist at Anne, although he usually fell down before he could hurt her. He'd start brawls in the street in the middle of the day in front of the entire neighbourhood. She thought she could handle it and they'd be OK in the end if she just got him through, and then he'd show up in front of her friends, blind drunk and soiling himself. She was a proud woman, but he broke her spirit.

Then one day she went to work and found that the bank had closed the salons – it turned out that John had a secret gambling habit and all their money was gone. She was only 30 at the time, with two kids, one in private school, and thought her life was over. Why had God sent her this kind of man again?

It was shortly after this that we had a chat and she told me, 'I've just woken up. I've been going to chapel for years and praying, and nothing has ever happened, but last Sunday I heard every word of the sermon for the first time. And I now I know it's *me* that's the problem in these relationships. Why do I need these men? Why am I attracting them?'

She was astute enough to realize that she was drawn to bad boys like John because she wanted to fix them in some motherly kind of way.

Realizing this left her with two choices: either she got out of the marriage with John, thanked her lucky stars for the realization and vowed to choose more wisely next time, or else she stepped aside and looked at the chaos, recognized her role in it, then plunged back in and tried to change it. If she left him she didn't know if she could be sure she'd pick the right man next time – after all, John had seemed like a good man and she could sometimes remember those qualities despite the booze. It was what lay underneath the drinking and the gambling that she had set out to fix, and that was his need for attention. He was just a big kid, and when he was 'naughty' and drank, Anne had to concentrate on him.

So she stuck with him and worked hard to help him through AA and to rebuild their business. In the end both of them ended up as counsellors for people with alcohol and debt problems, using their own experience to help other people out of the same traps. It could have gone another way – Anne really took on an incredibly hard life and John might not have had the courage to face his demons and get better. Things could have got much worse, but because they both realized what they had to do, they made it.

8

'Can Spirit Help Me Find Love?'

A couple of years ago I was invited to take part in a big spiritual event in a conference centre in Las Vegas. For several days there would be seminars, talks and parties and thousands of people would attend. I was scheduled to run a session called 'I Can Do It' and I found myself up on a platform in front of an audience of hundreds, bringing messages through from the spirit world and answering questions. A helper with a microphone was roaming the audience so that when someone wanted to ask a question, they could be heard by everyone.

The messages were coming through thick and fast when one very well-groomed lady who must have been in her late twenties stood up. The helper hurried over with the mike.

'I want to know,' she launched straight in, 'why my life is so bad. I'm unlucky. My sisters hate me and my mother won't even speak to me. My husband left me five years ago and I haven't had a serious boyfriend since. My relationships all seem to go wrong after a month.' I could hear the audience stirring in their seats as this laundry list went on. 'I've bought all the self-help books and I've done all the meditations and practices and I've said my prayers. I've asked for a man, I've done cosmic ordering and nothing has happened. Nothing! I'm still alone, nobody has come to me, my family hasn't made contact… Bad things happen to me. I think the universe has abandoned me. My life is a disaster.'

By now some people were calling out, 'Shut up!' and 'Sit down!' and we were in danger of the whole seminar breaking down. It was obvious that this woman needed some tough love.

'It's all right, everyone,' I called out. 'She's asked a question, so let's deal with it, because it probably affects a lot of people when you look at it on a bigger scale.'

I could see the lady puffing herself up a bit now that she had some attention.

'What brought you here today?' I asked. 'And why are you sitting here with me?'

'I don't actually know,' she replied. 'I just stumbled in here and thought you'd tell me something positive. I thought you might have a message for me from the other side.'

'OK, let's try and fix you, because your attitude is bad,' I said briskly, and everyone gasped because in America you're not supposed to tell people that sort of thing when you're being nice and spiritual. 'How many times have you said these things about how miserable your life is and how everyone hates you? Has anyone ever told you that you've behaved badly?'

She looked as though she was about to let loose another laundry list and this time it was going to be some pretty choice language aimed at me.

'Now hang on,' I said quickly, 'you want attention and you've got it now. The whole room is listening. Let's talk about your problems.'

'I did the practices,' the woman repeated, 'I asked for a man and I wrote down what he should be like and I did my positive thinking and he's not here.'

'You keep going on about this man. What man?'

'I want a man who'll love me for who I am. Who'll listen to me.'

Apparently she'd put in a request for some perfect bloke who must have been stored in a warehouse near Pluto or something, with his perfect tan, nice smile and willingness to listen. He probably gave foot rubs too! The trouble was, UPS didn't deliver ideal men, no matter how hard you thought positively about it, and you certainly couldn't order them from a catalogue.

Then she tried to rant about all the authors whose books she'd bought promising her this ideal man and how she wanted her money back, and I said, 'Don't blame them. You're the one who assumed it would work for you and if you go on like this you'll only go and find another guru and give them responsibility for your life. Unfortunately you walked into this room and I'm not going to cosmically order you anything. I'm going to order you to change yourself instead. And are you missing someone in your life? There's a man who's gone out of your life. Did your dad die?'

'Yeah, my dad died.'

'Were you young when it happened?' I wasn't acting as a medium at all here, it was just very obvious.

'Yeah.'

'And Daddy gave you lots of attention and Mummy never did when Daddy died?'

She looked affronted.

'I'm not being rude,' I assured her, 'but did you cry?'

'No, because it was all about my mother. I couldn't cry because she was supposed to be the special one.'

'That's you – since childhood you've had that hurt and you've been nursing it and making it worse. You've held that against your mother and she was probably grieving her husband at the same time as you were missing your father. Have you tried talking about this with your mother?'

'How can I? She hasn't spoken to me for ten years.'

'Have you tried talking to her?'

'No! She's the one who doesn't speak to *me*.'

'Do you think she really hates you or are you just assuming that? What kind of input have you had in your family's lives in these past ten years? Have you been there to offer love and support? Have you even phoned your sisters?'

Obviously not.

'Now, you're not a bad-looking woman,' I went on.

'I'm glad you think so.'

'No, you're not unattractive, but your attitude is awful and terribly off-putting. Is that how you greet people – by whining at them and telling them about your plight and that it's all terrible? Who in the universe are you trying to attract?'

'I just want someone who'll listen…'

'But what if you're no fun to listen to? If you were to love life and love the people around you, don't you think you'd deserve this ideal man a little more? He'd be more likely to notice you for a start than if you were just sitting at home waiting for your special delivery.'

'I suppose I don't really go out much.'

'And if you did, with a different attitude, don't you think your neighbour might be wondering where you'd been all his life? Why don't you try putting a bit more into loving other people and see where that gets you? Promise me you'll give your mum a call after the demonstration.'

She was quiet now and nodded and sat down, and I went on with the questions and answers.

What would it have been like if she'd tried to take her old attitude into a relationship? All that angst and hatred was just building up and yet she expected someone to love her in spite of it all. I expect that the bad behaviour had got her something in the past and she thought it might bring her something in the future. In the past she must have had some attention, of course, because of losing her father, but she'd clung to that and tried to make it the core of her life. This 'poor me' refrain had turned into a sadness that was sustaining itself and eating up all the parts of her life where she should have been growing as a soul, and she let it. She used her loss to gain attention. She didn't need a message from spirit, she needed to change at a very grounded level, by doing things, not by being lifted magically to a higher plane. The secret was within her, not the universe.

Meanwhile she was probably surrounded by people who could have used an extra friend, but by closing herself off and waiting for 'the universe' to end her problems, she was only shutting out the universe itself and thereby all her chances of meeting her ideal man! You do have to give fate a chance. It's not true that once you are open things will automatically come to you, but you won't wither away, you will blossom.

I didn't see the woman again until the end of the gathering in Las Vegas, when she appeared out of the crowd and gave me a big hug. 'I've spoken to my mom,' she told me.

She looked much happier, and I told her so. She started to thank me and I said, 'Look, all I did was answer your question the way any friend would have done. I just reflected back what you needed to hear.'

It turned out that after her performance at the seminar lots of people had come up to her to tell her about their experiences of cutting themselves off from loved ones and coming through it and having better lives now. All of a sudden she was attracting people who were nice – and all because she'd stopped putting up a front about how terrible her life was. To me, this was far more fruitful than getting through to her dad and having him say he loved her.

I think that before we can begin to have the relationships we dream of, we have to know ourselves and understand our own weaknesses and what we're looking for, as Anne and her husband did after they lost everything. That might happen before we get out of the front door and actually meet someone, like the woman in Las Vegas, or it might happen years down the line in a marriage, after the big blast of emotions at the beginning. And of course we can ask spirit for help in doing it. But we have to have clear eyes, not starry ones, if we're going to make a success of a relationship and really grow spiritually.

I do think, though, that if you're meant to meet a certain person, you will be given that chance, whether by some influence from spirit or by your own actions.

At important points in our lives, the opportunities will land on our paths.

9

Lessons in Love

The truth is that love's not about people, it's a constant, something that we move through as we grow spiritually – if we don't get stuck, like that woman in Las Vegas, or Helen and her unrequited love, or Dave, who tried to pretend he wasn't infatuated with a younger man. Not every relationship will work out, but if we accept the lessons learned without bitterness and move on, they can take us a step closer to a better love.

When I see people at the beginning of a relationship they're usually completely caught up in the passion and think that it'll be like that for the next 50 years. But that full force of romance can't be switched on 24/7 – imagine how exhausting that would be, and how little energy you'd have for the rest of your life and the people in it. But don't get scared that you'll lose something when the fires die down and the violin music stops. When the rituals start to go away – the dressing up, the minding your manners and being careful what impression you make – then you have to work, but the opportunity for love – not romance – is stronger than ever. My mother just lost my father after 63 years of marriage and they were chalk and cheese, but they still survived everything that life could throw at them and she told me only the other day, 'I even miss the fights – they kept us together.'

It's when we play around and become selfish and say, 'I want this or that from love,' that we pull away from the real thing. When we begin to put conditions on love, we restrict the amount of love we can have in our lives. We worry that if someone doesn't do something they don't love us, or that we love someone more than they love us, but when we do that, all we are doing is putting a measure on love, a limitation on it, when it could be a bigger, greater thing.

If we think love is our God-given right, it can hurt us. If we're lucky to be touched by love in this life it should inspire us to be loving, to bring out the best in ourselves, not make ourselves and others unhappy.

At its best and truest, whether in a partnership or a marriage or a friendship, love is supportive and compassionate. And if we're touched by love for a particular person, we get a sudden insight into someone who's been a stranger. That burst of energy and understanding is there to show us what we could experience with many more people – the friends we already have and the friends we will have.

Love divides more easily than we do – it doesn't have to be focused on one person all the time. You can genuinely become a loving person and care for a lot of people, and that's just what love can give us, if we choose to learn: a better understanding of everyone.

I'm most inspired by the people who can go through the darkest times and still grow spiritually. This story is one of the most exceptional examples I've come across.

Dronma and I were among the mediums working at a weekend seminar in a church in Harrogate and 30 or so Germans were taking part. As there are no Spiritualist churches in Germany, it's common for people to travel to the UK for talks and readings with mediums, and a lady called Doris Foster had set up the opportunity for people to come to Harrogate. She'd been born in Berlin but married an Englishman and lived most of her life in the UK – she said she'd always felt English because her mother had given her an English name.

The main hall of the church had ante-rooms on either side where we could give private readings and one of the people who came to see me there was a lovely woman called Sigi. I'll always remember how straightaway I was struck by her openness and her affection. People like that just radiate something incredible.

She sat down and I did my usual introduction, asking if she'd had a reading before and telling her not to give me too much information but to let it come from spirit, and she leaned over and took my hand and said gently, with a smile, 'I'm dying. I just want to know who's going to be waiting for me when my time comes. I'm not scared, so don't worry about me.'

All through the reading she had a beautiful calmness and paid plenty of attention, although I wondered what comfort spirit could bring to someone who was already so content in the face of adversity. She was pleased with the messages she got, though, and I was moved by the grace she showed.

We chatted a little afterwards and, without even thinking about it, I took off a little silver Celtic ring I was wearing and gave it to her. I just said, 'I want to give you a gift,' and she tried to demur and said, 'Oh, you don't need to do that.' But I felt compelled to do it and told her I knew there must be a reason for it, so she took it from me.

She left and I ran off to find Dronma and tell her the story. I met her halfway across the church in great excitement. 'I've just done a reading for a man who has cancer,' she said, 'and I gave him my ring. I don't know why. I just took it off and gave it to him.'

We knew the two people must be connected somehow and sure enough we turned to see them standing together and holding the rings, laughing and smiling. They told us their story – they were already married and both were dying of cancer, but they'd been debating whether to renew their vows and have a special blessing. Dronma and

I had unwittingly answered that question by providing the rings. What a sign.

Doris was a Spiritualist minister and they asked her for help in organizing a ceremony so they could make vows beyond death. They married again that weekend in the church and there wasn't a dry eye in the house – not out of sadness, but pure emotion. The vows were beautiful: 'I will love you every single day and cherish the precious moments of life we have left and be with you beyond death.' Whichever went first would wait for the other and gently help them over to the other side. But they swore not just to die, but to live.

A year later their daughter came along to a seminar I did in Dusseldorf and gave me back the rings. Her parents had both died within the year, but their last months had been like a honeymoon. They had gone off on a cruise, had little holidays here and there, done everything they wanted to do… She said, 'It was wonderful to watch them fall in love with each other all over again. They'd never lived like that until the last year.'

It had taken both of them having these terrible diagnoses to wake up and say, 'Enough is enough, let's enjoy the time we have left.' I remembered Sigi telling me it was a shame they'd had to learn such a simple lesson through such a devastating illness when they could have had 30 years of this love, not a few months, but she said she was glad she had woken up because the love they had now was so intense and so special. 'Maybe that's all we're allowed in this life,' she said, 'this short intensity of life and love...'

Maybe she was right. She was certainly somebody I really felt for and truly learned from – just imagine what character it takes to create such a big, positive and open an emotion as love when you've got a death sentence hanging over you. To find love while dying and to intensify it through that death is extraordinary, but perhaps we can own that every day of our lives if we let ourselves.

10

'Will I Win the Lottery?'

When word got out that I was learning to be a medium, it seemed as if every bloke who came into the barber's shop wanted me to turn my skills to something more profitable. They wanted to know which horse would win the fourth race that afternoon or what numbers were going to come up on the lottery. They were only half-joking most of the time, but there was no way I was going to help them out.

I did actually know a young couple from Liverpool who won the pools in the late seventies. A good wage was £25 a week at that time and they landed £4,000 with some lucky numbers and turned into the neighbourhood cash machine – they took everyone out and showered them with banknotes like confetti. They were the most popular punters in the local pub – drinks were on them every night. They had the best-dressed kids in the city and a bunch of daft ornaments on their shelves. They could have bought a flat with that cash, but it was all gone in three months – poof! – and all they had to show for it was a letter from the bank saying they had nothing left.

Maybe you've already guessed that once their windfall was blown, all their backslapping mates in the pub started to look awkward, and funnily enough there was nobody to buy them a drink as a thank you for all the handouts they'd had in those three heady months of the pools win. Those false friends just fell away.

I don't think there was much of a cosmic reason for them getting the money; it was just pure dumb luck. It was the aftermath of their spending spree that was significant, because that was where they really learned the meaning of the word 'value'.

Luck is a force which does affect our lives, but it's not something that we can control. It comes and goes, whether we hang a horseshoe over the front door or not, and it's very subjective. Were that Liverpool couple lucky to have lots of money for three months? It didn't change their lives in the end. Similarly, is it really bad luck if your car is stolen when it isn't insured? You still have your kids and your friends.

It's a matter of perspective: if one man loses ten million dollars and ends up with two million more than another man earns in a lifetime, is he unlucky? A lot of the things that people deem to be 'bad luck' aren't all that terrible really and if you have the grace to realize what's important in your life, you can accept that there will be ups and downs no matter what you do. If you want to win the lottery, perhaps you should ask yourself why.

What about creating your own luck? I knew a young man who was a serious gambler in his spare time and always reckoned that when he was doing well at work it was a 'good sign' that he should hit the bookie's or the casino. He'd gamble more and often win more on those occasions, and if he did lose, he claimed it was never 'much'. I think it was more likely that he just felt more confident then and was in too good a mood to get upset about losing some cash.

But it was also a matter of karma, which he was in tune with in a funny way. Simply put, he took action in a way that brought him good fortune – he never could have won if he hadn't taken part in the first place and given himself the chance to hold the winning ticket. The 'karmic probability' behind that is pretty straightforward!

And what about spirit? If we kiss the dice before we roll them and think of our gran, is she going to intervene and turn up a couple of sixes for us? Those in spirit can influence the flow of cash into and out of our lives, but they aren't some kind of munificent genie who will fulfil our wildest dreams of piles of pointless loot. Sometimes spirit holds us back from scooping up the banknotes. At other times there are pennies from heaven when we need them most.

When I was in my late twenties my Auntie Sylvia, who'd been a second mother to me, was dying. Her son Stephen had died of cancer when he was only a boy and she'd sort of adopted me afterwards. I hadn't seen much of her in my twenties because I had been too caught up in my marriage, sons and then separation, but when she was very ill I borrowed some money from Jim to fly down and see her in London. We were pretty broke at the time and wondering how we were going to shift our bills.

Sylvia, who was a very practical, down-to-earth woman, was busy setting her life to rights before she died and as I sat by her bed she told me that she'd decided she wanted me to be sole heir for her and her husband Michael. Now they'd done very well for themselves and it would have been a matter of several hundred thousand pounds, money which would have altered my life beyond recognition.

Sitting there, knowing I'd needed Jim's last pay packet for the journey, my instinct was to say, 'No, I don't want the money.' And even as I said it, my brain was thinking, 'What the hell's coming out of my mouth? Shut up!'

'You can't say that,' Sylvia said. 'You need that cash. Think what you can set up for your sons.'

And I still said no, even though I didn't know why.

I was with Sylvia for several days and she kept trying to bring the matter up, but I stayed firm. At the time I didn't have much cash of my own, but I was reckless with what I had. I'd just started my development as a medium and was getting a bird's-eye view of my own character for the first time and I thought that if I inherited that money at some unknown point in the future when Michael died, I would probably go out on the town and party or give it all away.

When Sylvia died, I went back to Glasgow and found Jim very upset. His own mother was very sick, even though she was only in her early sixties, and when I confided to him my regret that I hadn't spent more time with Sylvia, he admitted that the only thing he wanted now was to take his mum on a last holiday. We only had 15 quid between us at the time.

In *Stories from the Other Side* I gave an account of what happened next. As we were sitting in front of the telly I saw a roulette wheel in my mind's eye and the little white ball dropping, click, into the zero. It happened again, click. That was enough. I took the cash we had and drove to Chevalier Casino, hoping I wouldn't have trouble finding a parking space, as there was barely any fuel in the tank.

From there it all went like clockwork: a parking slot by the door, an empty roulette table just opposite the entrance and our £15 turning into £3,500 in the space of a half-hour. I hardly knew what I was doing, but the numbers kept coming up and I was soon stuffing my blazer pockets with chips.

When I got home I made Jim try to guess how much I'd won and he'd got as far as £500 when I took all the bills out of my pockets and threw them up in the air.

That £3,500 was enough – and no more – for a wonderful holiday for Jim and his mum and to shift our debts. Every single penny from heaven had a purpose – it wasn't pure luck, but something deeper than that.

Now in case you think I'm making myself out to be some kind of saint for turning down Sylvia's money and using the casino winnings for a noble purpose, I should tell you that later I found another £800 in chips in the pockets of my blazer and of course Jim and I thought we'd got it made. This would be our new way of making money – till we got banned from the casino. So back to the Chevalier we went and in five minutes we'd lost the lot. Talk about a lesson learned! We never returned to the casino after that.

Years later, when my Uncle Michael died in an accident, the family was shocked to discover that he and Sylvia had divided their money between everyone in the family apart from me. Because my uncle and aunt were extremely close to me, it seemed strange, but I knew it was what I'd talked over with Sylvia. She did have the last laugh, though. The lawyers handed over an envelope with my name on it that contained a cheque for £5,000 and a note from Sylvia saying, 'Have a bit of fun.'

One of my favourite tales of pennies that really did come from heaven came from a big brawny guy called Willie Stuart who used to come into the barber's shop to have his hair cut. He was a taxi driver and he liked to tease me about my mediumship because he was a good Catholic lad. 'So go on then, tell me how my haircut's going to turn out,' he'd say. I liked to give as good as I got and we always had a laugh.

One week he came in with a funny expression on his face and when he'd sat down and I'd tied the cape on him and asked him if he wanted his usual, he broke out, 'You know, I slag you lot off, but something's happened that I need to tell you about.'

'What's that then, Willie?' I asked, wondering if he was about to pull my leg again.

'I was skint last week,' he told me. 'There was no business and I didn't even have enough cash left to hire the cab for this week. I didn't know how I was going to get by if I missed a day's work and I didn't want to tell my wife. So – and I swear I never did this before – I sat down and I asked my mum for help. You know she died some years ago, but I said to her, "If you can help me, please guide me, because I'm really struggling."' The funny expression on his face was changing into a smile. 'And you'll never believe this – but you probably will because I bet this happens to you all the time – I went to the cemetery, as I do every Sunday, to take my mum some flowers, and I looked down at her grave and I did a double-take. I just couldn't believe it. Because there was a ball of banknotes there – as though someone had had it in their fist or pocket. Twenty quid notes. And it was only enough money for a week's cab hire, wasn't it?'

His eyes were streaming at this point and he was rocking back and forth in his chair and shaking with laughter. He knew he'd got his just deserts for teasing me and Christine about the mediumship. What better proof could he have? I did warn him, though, that after that little piece of evidence, as I knew from my experience in the casino, the cosmic cash register was probably closed.

11

'Is Money Bad for my Karma?'

I've got a friend who's become a successful, wealthy politician through years of hard work and skill. His wife called me a while ago because she was worried about him. She said he was out of control, spending money as if it was water and acting wildly. She asked me to do a reading for him, but when I went over to see him he was patronizing and dismissive. 'I don't need this,' he blustered, 'and why does my wife need to talk to you? She's got everything she could possibly want.'

One night I had a dream which seemed significant. In it my friend was in a casino and there was a shadow hanging over his head. He was chucking chips down on the table as though they were bird food.

The next day his wife phoned me in a panic because her husband had gone missing. He was supposed to be taking a train north on a work trip and calling her from his hotel when he got there, but the night had passed without her hearing from him.

I reassured her. 'This is going to sound weird, but he's fine. He went to a casino.'

'Why would he do that?' she said. 'How do you *know* that?'

'I'm telling you, he did. I wouldn't say it if I didn't feel strongly about it. You'll get a call from him in a minute.' And I told her about the dream.

She wondered what the shadow was, but I honestly didn't know. We rang off and she later told me that he had indeed phoned from a hotel with a casino where he'd gone after cancelling his original booking, but he hadn't told her about the money or the gambling.

His wife was disturbed by his behaviour. She'd long since realized that he was turning into a different man from the one she'd married – the man who'd had no money but who'd turn out his pockets to help someone begging in the street. 'He was the most generous man alive when he had nothing,' she told me, 'but this isn't him. It's as if he's delirious.'

The next time they were in London they came round to see me and I felt that he was no longer there – he was just an ego. We all had a long chat and his wife and I tried to get him to look at his real life – his kids, his marriage and his true friends – but he just dismissed us: 'Who are you to say this? You have no idea how important I am.'

'I'm pretty contented,' I said, 'and that's the most important thing, but you're out of control and you're not happy.'

'That's just bollocks!' he blustered.

His wife apologized.

A few days later I had another dream about him and his shadow and I could tell it was growing denser and darker.

A different man called me a month later – a broken one. He said he had to see me and sent a car round to pick me up.

When I got to his hotel I found him curled up on the floor in a foetal position, unable to move.

'What's happened to you?' I thought he must have been diagnosed with a terrible disease or lost a child.

'I've lost…' and here he named a big sum of money. He'd lost it in another casino.

'Did you ever *have* that much money?'

'What are you talking about? I had nearly twice as much as that!'

'I mean, did you ever really have it or was it just on paper? You probably haven't really lost anything. I bet you'll get it back. You could never have spent that much money anyway, even if it was in your wallet.'

'Look, I've got a meeting to go to. But I can't go. I just can't.'

At this point his wife walked in, completely unperturbed. I asked her if she was all right and she assured me that she was absolutely fine. 'He thinks this is important. It's not important, this is what we've been fighting over for months. The kids and I are important, not this. We've got more than enough money left, we'll never be poor.'

'I can't show my face in public,' he groaned. 'Everyone will know what happened to me.'

'Come on, you've got a meeting to go to,' I told him. 'Stand up and be a man.'

'Is my shadow still with me?'

'Probably not – you've had to face it and this is it.'

The only thing I could do was offer him a healing. After that, his wife and I got him off the floor between us and away to the meeting.

She called me later to say that he'd survived it but now he'd crumpled again. I asked her again if she was OK. 'Oh, I'm fine. I just step over him,' she said. 'This is a real wake-up call for him. I think he was waiting for the money to mean something to him, just chucking away the chips in the casino like that. And now it does. He thinks he's lost face, but he'd already lost it when he started throwing money around.'

She's waiting for the man she married to come back to the relationship now, and he's lucky to have her because she can remember what he was before he lost his head. She knows he's a good man and he just has to remember that.

There's nothing intrinsically bad about money in any quantity, it's what happens to us that's important. If we're not careful and don't have our own inner balance to check us, we can be shaped by it. And at best it can create wonderful things, but at worst it can destroy.

Money is like ego – when it's out of control, you're the last one to realize it. You need to be sure there's a reason for you having it, so you can qualify what you're doing and use it properly, not to light your cigars when you don't even like cigars!

In my work I've met several celebrities at the height of a sudden burst of success and just raking in the money. Like that young couple in Liverpool, they seemed to have lost any idea of how much that money was actually worth – they couldn't think as far as the next day. Because they weren't paying attention to what was really going on around them or inside them, the money was allowed to become a malevolent energy. It attracted false friends who went into a kind of feeding frenzy and stripped them bare, or people who were afraid to tell them what was really happening in both their bank accounts and their careers.

Money can also wake up desires that have lain dormant. I remember Darren Day telling me he'd snorted or swilled down hundreds of thousands of pounds in drugs and booze – the money had given those weaknesses free rein. He woke up one morning in the gutter outside a theatre in the West End that had his name up in lights and knew he'd hit rock bottom. He'd lost not only his money but also his talent and his path in life, alienating his ex-partner Suzanne and almost jeopardizing his chance to be a father to their son Corey.

Money is an energy and it can be a good thing, but there are limits to what you can actually hold in your hands and understand. In our current life there's only so much we can harness. But money can have real meaning when you *give* it that meaning and you use it to do things which will truly enhance your life and the lives of other people.

I've never seen the human spirit stronger than in South Africa, where the kids I met in Soweto had absolutely nothing and lived surrounded by horrific crime and yet radiated joy. The thought of them still lifts me. That's a different attitude to life – they take huge pleasure in what little they have. It doesn't mean they're not ambitious or that they live in a magical pixie land where they don't know the value of money – they do, acutely. They know that money will feed you, clothe you, educate you, put a roof over your head and help you travel the world – above all, enable you to do concrete and practical things and help others as well as your family. They don't look to it for *spiritual* happiness, though – they generate that themselves.

If you don't grow with your cash pile, you'll just be adding extra zeros to your bank balance, not your soul. The energy that money provides can turn you into a type of junkie.

I think back to a man called Ian who was another part of the hairdressing community in Glasgow. He was a great guy, always wanted to buy a drink for everyone when the day was over and loved a sing-a-long in the pub. It was common for one or another of us to be short of cash and someone would always lend you a tenner, but this guy wouldn't expect to see it back. We lived in a part of town where nobody locked their doors because they didn't have anything to steal. The pensioners would leave their doors open so you could pop in and see if they were OK and if they wanted something from the shops. People were very open and they looked out for one another. There was a real camaraderie between the barbers and hairdressers and Ian was at the centre of that. He was no saint and he liked the odd trip to the bookie's, but you couldn't throw a party without someone asking if he'd be there. If you could guarantee he was in the house, you'd always have a great turnout. He brought a really benevolent energy with him.

He took the chance to set up his own business and it took off like a rocket. Normally it took a while to build up clientèle, but in his case it seemed no time at all before he was taking on more staff and opening up other branches. We knew he'd wanted it for years, so we were really pleased for him.

The trouble was, Ian started to change. He stopped coming out to the pub and the bookie's. Soon you'd ask someone if they'd seen him out socializing and they'd look blank. No one had had a drink with him for months and he wasn't interested in going to parties.

When I bumped into him, it wasn't hard to see why. He looked physically different, worn down and angry. I tried to chat with him and he was downright nasty. I asked him how the salons were going and he snapped, 'It's none of your business,' then shut down the conversation. Someone else told me they'd asked him to lend them a tenner and they'd thought he was going to kill them. Another friend dropped into his salon one day to say hello and found the staff looking boot-faced – Ian had disappeared out the back when he saw his old friend coming and told them to say he was out.

As time went on he became a kind of hermit. It was obvious that he thought that everyone was after his money or a job, and even though he was only in his fifties he looked decades older.

I passed him in the street once and tried again. I couldn't help but say he was looking rough.

'No wonder,' he muttered, 'with all the worries I have. If only you knew the pressure I'm under.'

'What worries? The business is doing well and you've just got back from holiday.'

'You talk a lot of rubbish, that shit you do with the spirits. You can't read me.'

'I'm only chatting to you as a friend. What happened? You were a nice guy.'

'That's shit.'

His own greed was consuming him, the money suffocating him; I could see him going under. Soon he was blanking everyone in his life. His daughter emigrated to Canada, partly, I heard, because she couldn't cope with her father any more, and his son disowned him. If money is an energy, he overdosed on it and it brought him no joy. He could only think about making more and defending it from all those 'former friends' who were just out for cash.

He died only six or seven years after he got his own business. He had cancer but died only weeks after being diagnosed. What a waste of a good man, a man who knew how to appreciate life until he had success that terrified him.

I remembered Ian when I met a woman in a bar in France, years later, who'd been through the worst but had a greater understanding of money's energy than Ian ever managed. Jim and I popped in for a drink one evening and struck up a conversation with her. She was just one of those people whose life fascinates you. She was the manager, and she had a face that looked as though she'd really been through hard times, but she was an open soul. She told us she'd been born into a very wealthy family in England and she'd had a rich husband, a big house, everything she wanted. She'd also had booze and other drug addictions and a breakdown which saw her stuck in a private hospital for two years. She owed her dealers masses of money, couldn't pay her bills and was bankrupt. When she left hospital she ran away, and that was how she'd fetched up in that bar.

Now she had a job and a bit of a wage, and she was happy. It wasn't an impressive bar, but she'd never had anything as grounding as a job before and she felt that she was finally seeing real life and meeting real people. She knew that a relative of hers had died and that lawyers were trying to contact her because he'd left her a fortune, but there was no way she was going back to that life. She'd changed her name and hoped they never found her.

'It would be hell to go back,' she told us. 'I've been in the middle of all that greed and materialism before and I didn't have any control over it. I know it wouldn't be long before I was lost again. That money is a beast, not a blessing.'

I suppose you could say that that woman had chosen to take those drugs or run up those debts and that she should take the opportunity to take control of her old life rather than run away from it, but sometimes recognizing your limits is the best way of taking control. Now she was playing safe and simply wouldn't put herself in the way of temptation.

Because she'd been through so much she could recognize when others were struggling and we saw her on other nights that holiday taking someone aside and trying to find out what the real problem was. It seemed that she'd helped a lot of other lost souls who had turned up in that place.

What was interesting was that when she kicked her drink and drug addictions she also weaned herself off the money that had made a junkie out of my old friend Ian. It could have made a lot of things easier for her, but she'd found a richness in that bar, weird though it sounds for a recovering alcoholic. She told us she'd never felt alive and part of something before she got there. She'd learned the hard way how to count her blessings and be thankful for them every day and her new life was far richer than the old one as a result.

Money – whether it's a windfall or a sudden loss that empties your pockets – often marks the fork in the road. The path we thought we were happily following might split in two or even crumble away at our feet. When I turned down the inheritance from Sylvia, I set myself on one course of action. Who knows what would have happened to me if I'd taken it instead? What if my friend the politician had doubled his money at the casino instead of losing it? Would that have been a wake-up call as loud as the one he had when he faced his shadow and lost the millions?

I've had people ask me questions like, 'Will my daughter marry well?' and I've had to turn the question back on them and say, 'What do you mean by "well"?' Do they want her to be rich in spirit and in friends or to have a Lamborghini and a husband who's got three girlfriends on the side? The word 'wealth' can be applied to many things.

I was doing a week's stretch as a tutor at the Spiritualist church's Arthur Findlay College near Stansted when I met a woman called Mrs Carey. We liked to have a morning cigarette and a cup of coffee in the bar every day and set the world to rights. She must have been in her sixties, a good-looking confident woman who you could tell was very assured in her spiritual life. She ran a shop which sold candles and other knick-knacks, and I noticed her partly because she seemed so self-reliant. She was always wandering off to steal some time for herself pottering round the gardens or quietly taking everything in. The college was in Stansted Hall, a nineteenth-century manor on the site of a much older house, and the gardens were beautifully maintained, stretching off as far as the eye could see in every direction. Mrs Carey seemed to relish the peaceful atmosphere and I'd often see her out contemplating the magnificent tulip tree in the middle of the main lawn.

She didn't take much prompting to tell me the story that had led her to that quiet contentment. She had originally been married to a well-to-do businessman and they'd had quite the life, with a big posh house with all the nicest fixtures and fittings and a new car every year. She was her husband's secretary but she had plenty of time to have coffee and cake with the local ladies and feel very much part of the smart set.

Her pleasant existence was shattered when she discovered that her husband had been having an affair with her own sister. She left him and exiled herself to a tiny studio apartment while her sister moved in with her ex-husband. The next seven years were purgatory as she muddled along in a low-paid job and ate her heart out alone every night in the little flat. She felt ugly and worthless and started to eat huge amounts of food and put on weight, thinking it didn't matter because she was repulsive anyway. She thought she was in mourning for her marriage, but one day she suddenly realized that it wasn't her husband she missed but her nice lifestyle. She'd been crying over the loss of her big house and her coffee with the posh ladies, not him.

Then her father died and she knew that she would have to face her sister and her ex-husband at the funeral. She got the shock of her life as they stood facing each other across the grave and she realized that her sister was an alcoholic and drunk already that day and that her husband seemed to have withered away to nothing. Her eyes were opened – there she was, in good health, in good spirits really, and look at the destruction that that nice wealthy lifestyle had wrought on them! *She* could have been that other woman in the churchyard, tottering around and stinking of booze.

That was her turning point. She decided what she wanted to do with her life and went about setting up her shop. She got her eating back under control and started exercising more, and gradually the weight dropped off. A little way down the line, she started to go out with one of the sales reps who did business with her and they fell in love and married. She became that self-confident woman who'd impressed me so much at the teaching week because, she told me, 'I'm not rich, but I've got enough contentment to last me for the rest of my life. People look for wealth in all the wrong places. They pray to angels and gods and all sorts of things for cash. But the riches of this Earth come from this Earth, and we just need to know where to find them.'

So what's the best way to deal with money? I think it's to run two bank accounts, a material one and a spiritual one, and keep a good balance in both. Louise Hay told me when I first joined Hay House, 'When you're wise enough to distribute wealth with proper compassion, then that money will come to you. First you have to learn to use it to do what feels right.' Those are words I always try to keep in mind. When you're worthy of money, it'll come to you and you won't be destabilized by it.

You may also find that as you develop spiritually you'll require less and less materially from the universe. You'll be the one giving things away and using your money to make things happen for other people. Use that energy well.

12

'Is Death a Punishment?'

I was working in the salon one day when one of the girls answered the phone and said it was for me. I apologized to my customer and went to take it. A woman with a rather strange cut-glass accent was on the line. She announced her name, Sonia, and that she was on her way to see me. I started to protest that I was booked up for the afternoon, but she just brushed me off and said, 'I'll see you soon.'

I'd just put the phone down when a man walked into the salon with a tray of cakes from one of the best patisseries in Glasgow and said, 'Are you Gordon Smith?'

I was asking him what was going on when the most glamorous woman swept in, all big hair and fur coat. 'Hello, darling, it's me, Sonia!' she said. 'You're going to help me take the pain away.'

'Who on earth are you?'

There was no getting her out of the shop, so I told her she'd have to wait while I finished my client. She just about managed it. All the time she kept talking in the funny accent that I couldn't place – it wasn't quite American or posh English.

Finally we put the kettle on and took a cake each and went into the kitchen out the back so that I could give her a reading.

Straightaway a teenage boy came through – her son – and it was as though her whole façade, the big coat and hair and accent, fell away.

'Is he happy?' she asked in broad Glaswegian. 'Is he all right?'

'He's in a good place now. He's showing me what happened. He got caught in a fight. It was nothing to do with him.'

The lad had been having a drink after work when a fight had started up nearby and when he'd tried to intervene he'd been stabbed.

'Are you sure he's OK?' she insisted.

'Positive. He's saying he loves you. Don't worry.'

When the reading was over she wanted to talk more about what had happened to her son. She'd forced herself to go and identify his body and insisted on pulling back the sheet that covered him, only to discover that he'd been stabbed not just once but over and over again.

'Those animals – they'd never even met him!' she spat. 'They didn't have any history with him – how could they do that to him? Go on doing it again and again?'

After a while she wiped her eyes, pulled her coat back on, put her fabulous façade into place and off she went. I thought that was that, although I didn't feel she'd got much peace of mind, but a few weeks later the phone rang and I recognized her voice, though she didn't even bother with the fancy accent this time.

'I need to see you again. I've done some pretty bad things.'

'What kind of bad things?'

'Oh, I couldn't tell you, but they're bad. I think that's why my son was taken from me. It was my fault.'

'No, God didn't take him away from you as a punishment, he was just in the wrong place at the wrong time, and you weren't even there, so how could you have saved him? Why is it that you want responsibility for that?'

Then she started to tell me. She'd been a thief and though she'd never harmed a single person physically, she'd stolen from some big companies.

'How many years has your boy been dead?'

'Seven.'

'You've spent seven years thinking that stealing those things murdered your son? Blaming yourself?'

'Yeah…'

'But did those things belong to someone who valued them? Or were they just stock in a shop? There's something else wrong here – there's something from your childhood, where someone's said you were a bad girl. Who told you that and made you think that it would come back to haunt you?'

She didn't have an answer for that, so I went on, 'You know, those things you stole didn't really affect other people. It might have been against the law, but how would that match losing your own son?'

I couldn't for the life of me make her see that there wasn't a link between the stolen goods and the way that her son had been taken from her. The thing was, she'd meant the boy to make up for all her own mistakes, giving him an expensive education and making him into a perfect son – handsome, charming, polite. Her golden boy had been her attempt to escape her old self. When he died she was probably already set up to think she was responsible, already feeling guilty for what she'd done in the past. She'd made a kind of false karma for herself and let it make her suffering darker.

You can make a punishment monster that is bigger than you and out of your control. Remorse and guilt go into it, along with the need to beat yourself up. That's what happened to my friend in the fur coat. She had lost the one thing she loved more than life itself and she saw that as her wake-up call, but she could have woken up at any time without her son being lost.

A lot of people who come to me for a reading have already taken on the idea that a death is their fault. It's like the folk who think they're being hurt because they have too much money. They look downtrodden and defeated – they have plucked something out of their past that they feel guilty over and they're convinced it's connected to what their loved one went through.

In some ways, it's the easiest thing in the world to do. It's natural to look at the loss of a loved one and want answers to impossible questions like 'Why them? Why now?' And if, like Sonia, guilt and self-loathing are already there inside you, the next question is bound to be: 'Is it my fault?'

The thing to keep in mind is that *death doesn't have to make sense*. You don't lose a son because you stole a diamond necklace or because you made a million. A murderer doesn't get his 'just deserts' when he is killed in a car crash years after his crime. A charity worker doesn't get cancer because 'Only the good die young.' If you think that, you're coming at it from the wrong angle. Wouldn't that mean that an apple-cheeked nun of 95 was evil? Or that your great granddad made it to 80 because he was no use to anyone?

So much of our fear of death – and therefore of living – comes from the notion that death is a punishment, but it is part of the world and will come to us all sooner or later. You don't get cancer because you were nasty to your little brother, you get it because it exists. There is such a thing as being unlucky without generating that bad luck for yourself. I'll say again, you can't control everything that will happen in this world. Sometimes the best you can do is to see yourself as clearing some of the darkness for others. There are dark forces at work in this world, forces which exist because of human behaviour and the stains and memories left behind from terrible events. But they are not caused by their victims.

Also, no matter how good you are, you can still be affected by that greater system of karma which runs parallel to our lives and can sweep us away like a tsunami. If a man happens to go into a tube station, for example, and there's a suicide bomber there who chooses that moment to set off the bomb and the man loses a limb, it may be that he walked into a bigger karma, something that he is perhaps somehow linked to. But it isn't a punishment because he made his girlfriend cry the other week.

At a recent book reading, a woman in the audience asked me if, when we died, we had to balance out our lives in some kind of day of reckoning. That's pretty true, although it doesn't involve being condemned to the fiery pits of hell and all that. The spirit world isn't a place of punishment. I've never had a communication from a spirit who was in hell or limbo. The spirit world is a bigger place than that, a place where energies meet and knowledge is shared. The experience is one of awareness, not retribution.

When you pass, you re-experience the most important moments of your life and see the consequences that resulted from your choices and how they affected other people. There's a kind of process of enlightenment where you see the patterns and purposes of your life laid clear, why you chose a certain course of action and what you have learned from those experiences.

If in this existence you're conscious of the things you have done and their outcome, then you get a head start in the spirit world and in any future existences. If you're less aware, then it will take you longer to learn those lessons, but you will still have the chance. Some of the 'heaviest' spirits I've received communications from were those who were lost in a fog of depression in life or who had committed really bad crimes in blind ignorance of the pain they were inflicting on others. It will take them more spiritual effort to reach that understanding of the bigger picture that will liberate them.

If we look at it from the point of view of spirit, death is a release from the confinement of this life and the lessons we've been having to learn the hard way. I called it a 'eureka moment' because it seems fitting – I get a great sense of joy and lightness from most spirits who have recently passed over. When you start to understand this transition to spirit and what it means for us, death doesn't seem so harsh.

They say religion is for people who are worried about going to hell, Spiritualism is for people who have already been dragged through it. Hell happens here on Earth: it's only as humans that we suffer, as spirits can't feel the same pain that we feel in human form. We should see our bodies as vehicles in which we're travelling, ones that will suffer wear and tear and be damaged by the things they come into contact with but are ultimately just shells for our soul. We are travelling through this world and when our journey is over we carry on back to spirit.

This is a story about a woman who felt she was being punished by someone on the other side but who ultimately found peace.

I arrived at a church in the Midlands about ten years ago to do a demonstration and was shown into what you might call the mediums' dressing room to put my stuff down and have a cup of tea. I was joined by a woman who was the church secretary and as we chatted she said, 'I think I've heard that you were friends with Albert Best?'

'Yes, I was,' I said.

'You know, that man saved my life,' she said.

I asked her to tell me what had happened.

Years ago she had been driving her car in Leicestershire, where she lived at the time, when a little girl had raced out in front of her wheels. The child was killed instantly and the woman saw it all unfold before her – the injuries, the screams, the shock. Although it wasn't her fault, she couldn't shift the horror from her mind and again and again she saw the child run out, felt the impact and saw the blood. Months and then a year went by in this fashion. She stopped eating, not caring if she could function or not, only wanting to dissolve. She didn't sleep because when she closed her eyes she saw the accident yet again. She was suicidal and one night in her bedroom she just screamed out, 'Why me? Why me? I hadn't done anything wrong!' and broke into sobs.

The following day she was walking through the town centre and she passed a building she'd walked by many times in her life without registering what it was: the Spiritualist church on Vaughan Way. She saw a poster saying, 'Internationally renowned medium Albert Best will be appearing here today at 2.30 p.m.,' and she turned and walked into the church as though there was a thread drawing her in. She took a seat and sat there dully, listening but barely able to focus. In fact she could hardly understand a word the little Ulsterman was saying.

Then he turned and pointed to her. It was a typically blunt Albert message.

'You killed a child a year ago,' he said, and gave the name of the street where it had happened. The whole church turned to look at her in horror. 'This child was with you last night,' Albert went on, 'when you were screaming out in your bedroom, "Why me, why me?"'

The woman freaked out, feeling as though she was under attack, her mind racing with questions as Albert produced more and more evidence: the age of the child, details of the car, the registration number… How could this strange man know the secret she was carrying about with her? How could he describe the way she was sitting in a darkened room, screaming to God, crying for death to come to her?

Albert went on to tell her that the little girl was there at that moment and that she had dragged the woman into the church. The fact that she was trying to kill herself connected her to that child, and the child needed her to get over it so she could move on on the other side, not be caught in an endless replay of her last moments.

'I want you to forgive yourself,' the girl said, through Albert. 'I cannot bear to watch you suffering.'

Twenty years later in the mediums' room in Nuneaton, the woman told me that those words had brought about a complete change in her. Now she could stop being haunted by memories and move on. Once she knew that the little girl was at peace, she herself found peace and started to live again. After her experience at the church she went on to investigate Spiritualism and later became part of the movement.

Even in the depths of the worst pain we can find a way to grow spiritually. It is natural to suffer emotional turmoil in the aftermath of a shock, but when we come through that, if we do not drag ourselves down with thoughts about being punished we can raise our mind to a higher spiritual frequency and learn from that experience and grow.

13

'What Is an Act of God?'

I learned a great lesson about nature one January, when Jim, our friend Gordon and I went on an out-of-season cruise round the Canary Islands. Out in the middle of the Atlantic the ship was hit by a force-nine gale with waves 30 feet tall and so violent that people had to cling on to furniture to keep themselves from being thrown all over the boat. Everything that could be secured or put into a drawer or cupboard was packed away in case it was thrown across a cabin and knocked someone unconscious. When the ship plunged down a wave, the bow was underwater, the propeller threshing in clear air and then smacking down onto the waves with an almighty crash. The top decks were shut and the ship battened down and we were all ordered to our cabins. Nobody could even walk to get to the infirmary and the nurse herself was prostrate with seasickness.

I think the passengers on that ship must have prayed to every god in the universe in those first few hours. Praying was about all you could do as you clung on and were tossed about by the force of the storm. One elderly man had a heart attack and plenty of others went into fits of hyperventilation when they weren't retching up on empty stomachs.

Poor Gordon had a cabin high up at the front of the ship, which was like riding on a big dipper for 30 hours. Jim and I were right in the guts of the liner, by the propellers, and as the ship listed for 12 hours through the giant waves, we realized that if she went down we'd have no chance. Even if we made it to the muster station with our life jackets, there was no way a helicopter could come and pluck us all off the ship, and once in the water we'd perish in less than an hour in the Atlantic midwinter. We were stone-cold helpless. To heck with it, we decided, we'd go down with the ship. We sat on the floor cross-legged, clinging to the fixed furniture, and opened a bottle of Scotch to numb ourselves.

The strange thing was, no matter how huge the sea and how dizzy and disorientated you were to begin with, you got used to it. For hours your mind ran through scenarios – 'What if we hit rocks? What if we capsize?' – and then after a while you stopped praying for life and prayed for death instead. You were alert to every new shudder in the sides of the cabin or groan from the engine, wondering what had changed and what it meant.

After 12 hours we could get up and stagger around the gangways, but it was like the *Marie Celeste*. Everyone was beyond seasickness – every part of their body as disorientated as if they'd been on spin cycle in a giant washing machine. Now we were on a swell, which was as nightmarish in its own way as the storm waves. The ship had had its anchor ripped away and we had to sail round Madeira for another 18 hours before the swell died down and it was safe enough to turn into the harbour.

I remember as a child hearing people say that the victims of storms or avalanches or earthquakes were killed by 'an act of God' but after that storm I understood that these things were nothing to do with God, but an act of the Earth. If the sea had wanted to destroy us, then it would have done it and there would have been nothing we could have done about it. When you place yourself in the belly of that element, you cede control of your fate.

God hadn't put some kind of hit out on all the hundreds of people on that ship, it was just the Earth acting on its own undercurrents and rhythms. We were irrelevant. The storm would have happened whether we had been there or not, and the liner would have been swallowed in an instant if it had tipped the wrong way down a wave. I've never felt so small or so powerless in my whole life.

Whenever I've come across people who've lost a loved one in a natural disaster they seem to have taken it personally. 'Why didn't we see it coming?' they ask, as though people go on cruises expecting a force-nine gale or take up skiing to experience an avalanche. It *is* personal in a sense, though, because not only have you lost someone but you've also realized how tiny and helpless you are in the face of both nature and fate. Even if you were with the person who died, you were unable to hold back the waves or the rockfall. So it's no surprise that after natural disasters people frequently either lose their faith or become more passionately devoted to it.

I've written before about a reading I did in Italy for a couple who lost a son in an avalanche when he was on a school skiing trip. I was surprised when not one but three children came through for them: their son, their niece and their son's best friend. For an hour and a half I brought through messages from those children about the little touches the parents had added to their funerals, about gestures they'd made or times they remembered. I tried to convey how happy they were now, but the man and woman wouldn't accept it. They were more well-to-do than the other families at the school and had paid for their niece and their son's best friend to go on the trip and now they wanted blame – they actually wanted their son to be angry with them.

'God was punishing us for being successful,' they said. 'That's why he took the children.' I tried to protest, but they wouldn't have it. 'Tell us, should we give our money away? Will that be a penance?'

They were also worried because God hadn't given them any kind of warning. Was that because they weren't 'good' enough?

I was sorry for these people. They were desperately seeking to make sense of what had happened and I tried to help them, but as the sitting went on and they got more and more overwrought I felt as though we were having a tug of war, with me and the children in spirit trying to drag them out of hell and them dragging us into it. All that guilt was 100 per cent self-inflicted – none of the other parents blamed them – and really they were trying to take responsibility for a force of nature. Sure, they could give their money away, but it wouldn't stop avalanches from happening in the future or people being killed.

Loss is not a matter of guilt or responsibility, it's just a harrowing emotion. But it is always made easier if you can accept that what happened was out of your control and focus on going forward and living your life.

14

'What Triggers a Violent Death?'

Before I started training as a hairdresser I worked in a builders' merchants in south Glasgow, loading vans and being a general dogsbody. Another 16-year-old lad called Michael worked with me, but he had a plan to get out – he was only working there until he was 17 and could enlist in the army. He went off in 1979 and the next time I saw him was after his training when he came back to the yard in his uniform, showing off a little and being really proud.

In the early 1990s, when I was working in a little church in Glasgow, I was approached by an elderly couple, tiny and hunched over, with a haunted look to them. 'You knew our son Michael,' they said. 'You used to work with him.' For a while I couldn't work out who they meant – I was trying to think of a barber or a hairdresser and then they named the builders' merchants and the penny dropped.

Michael had been killed in an IRA bombing in the early 1980s, although he hadn't even been in uniform at the time. His sister had been getting married and his parents had insisted he got leave to be at the wedding. He had been on his way to his return transport when the blast had gone off. He hadn't stood a chance.

His parents had become Spiritualists and had had several messages from him over the years, but his dad was still devastated and wanted to hear more evidence. He remained beside himself, convinced that by pushing Michael to get leave at that time he was responsible for putting that timeline into action.

What he needed to understand was where that timeline began – with the terrorists who made the decision to make a bomb and place it on the street. Whether it took them six months, a year or two years to do that, the process had begun, and the people who would be walking down that road where already on a timeline to be there at that time. Michael's sister's wedding and his father had nothing to do with it.

I was giving readings through an interpreter at a friend's house in Italy late in 2001 when a middle-aged couple were shown into the room. You didn't need to tune into spirit to see that they had suffered a great loss. They were like two empty shells. I explained through my interpreter what would happen and then we sat down and began.

'I've got a beautiful young woman here with me,' I said, and gave them a name, watching as they exchanged glances and then relaxed with the surprise, as if they'd hoped to hear from her but hadn't dared to believe she would really come through. 'She says she's with her grandmother and grandfather and she's safe and happy.' She also gave evidence that she was aware of things they'd done to change their home around and where they'd placed pictures of her. This was normal enough as a message, but then she began to impress what had happened on me.

She had been running in a crowd of people, trying to get somewhere safe, with a feeling of great fear and panic all round her, and then it had all gone dark, but I could feel that she was still running, and then she ran out of the darkness and into the light. I saw the Statue of Liberty and the skyscrapers of Manhattan and realized she must have died on September 11th in the World Trade Center. She left me with that sense of having come through darkness into light, and when her parents confirmed that she had indeed been one of the few Italian victims of 9/11, I did my best to convey that feeling of now being in a bright, open space. She didn't remember anything about the actual moment of her death.

Once, in a communication from Chi, I learned that when a physical body is badly broken, the etheric part, the soul, feels no pain, and that was exactly the sense that I got from this young woman in spirit: she had switched so quickly between the two states that she was unaware that she had even lost her body.

Her parents were hugely relieved to know that she wasn't suffering and that she was still with them – they'd become obsessed with the idea that her spirit was somehow trapped in America, far away from them.

'I'm with my friend,' she told them, naming a girl she'd been travelling with. I afterwards learned that after the two girls' deaths the two sets of parents had been drawn together in their grief. The parents in front of me were almost as delighted to get news of their friends' daughter as they were to hear from their own, the bond was now so strong between them. They promised they would share the recording of the reading with their friends.

They told me that their daughter had been visiting the Twin Towers as a tourist and she and her friend had been due to go on 10 September, but had changed their plans. Fate can work that way – one day you make a decision and you don't realize that it will take your life. How innocuous was it to say on 10 September 2001, 'Let's visit the World Trade Center tomorrow instead'?

We can string together the events that led to someone being killed in an accident or by the hand of another and see how everything seemed inevitable, but you have to know where that action began, otherwise you will complicate something quite simple. This girl and Michael both died because of plans made by terrorists, not because they chose a particular day to go to a certain site.

My own family went through a tragedy that showed me just how many choices an individual can make on the path to their fate and how helpless they are as they make those decisions. My aunt Frances had gone to visit one of her sisters and they had argued. Frances had stormed out, grabbing her coat as she left. When she got to her own flat she felt in her pockets for her keys and her purse and realized that she'd taken her sister's coat by mistake – they had bought identical ones. She tried to call her brother for help in getting into her home, but his phone was broken that night. She started walking back towards his house, but a private taxi pulled up and offered her a ride. That taxi driver raped and murdered her and her body was found shortly afterwards, dumped in the countryside. One simple action, taking the right coat, would have seen her safely home that night. As it was, both her family and the family of the killer, when he was caught, had their worlds turned upside down and were plunged into darkness.

When you go beyond the loss and try to extend the karmic logic, it gets sticky. Her sister might have felt overcome with guilt for arguing with her, or her brother for not getting his phone fixed that day, but how could either of them have known that that driver would be out on the streets that night? And what if she'd got another cab?

There were so many possibilities in that scenario, but I believe something kicked in and drew her to that man, and that to me is the karmic cycle. When you have a karmic link like that, you will follow it to the end. I'm sure there was a moment when she was about to leave her sister's house when she thought, 'No, I don't want to do this,' but when it's your destiny you're just driven, so she went on.

But how does that explain the stories of people who seem to have been snatched away from a terrible ending at the last minute? Is that 'cheating destiny'?

I was doing a workshop on mediumship when this subject came up. At such events people often come forward with their own experiences, but I wasn't prepared for the tale that one of the women present shared with us.

She and her husband lived in London and used to travel to work together on the tube. Every day they would walk to the station, take the escalator and walk onto the platform to take the train. One day they got to the top of the escalator and her husband suddenly stopped and said, 'I need to get some cigarettes.'

'Why get them now?' she asked him. 'Can't you get them in your lunch break?'

'I can't do that, there are no shops near the office.'

She was really annoyed. 'We'll miss the train and be late for work!'

But he was insistent: 'If I don't get a pack of fags now, I'll never get them.'

Infuriated, she stood there tapping her feet while he went off to queue at the newsagent's.

It was 7 July 2005 and while he was in the queue, waiting for his 20 pack, a suicide bomber detonated explosives in his rucksack on the train they would have caught – the train they always caught.

You could say those cigarettes saved their lives, but it's more likely that it just wasn't their time to go. He might have thought he was lured away from the escalator by the need for nicotine, but the force of their destiny was more insistent than nicotine cravings. At the time, of course, they weren't even aware that this was a type of precognition: all he knew was that he absolutely had to buy that packet of fags!

How many people get that flash of warning? What's certain is that if it's not your time to go, however that warning presents itself to you there's no chance that you will miss it.

I was giving a demonstration of mediumship in Wales, and one of the messages I brought through was for a woman who seemed at first glance to be very old. 'This is a message from a little girl who went to school one day and didn't come back,' I said. 'I understand that this happened a long time ago. She's a happy wee girl and she's with her friends' – here I gave the names – 'and she wants you to stop blaming yourself, because it's awful to see.'

The lady in the audience didn't say anything, but I could see her shaking and crying. Her daughter only wanted to get through to her to lighten her mind, but because the woman obviously couldn't accept this, I stopped the reading and called out to her that it would be better if I talked to her privately afterwards.

When the demonstration was over I saw her waiting for me, a tiny, frail woman, although now that I was closer I noticed that her eyes were younger than I'd thought – something had beaten her down physically. We went to a private room and I sat her down to go on with the reading and she said, 'My daughter died in Aberfan.'

On 21 October 1966 the little girl had been in her classroom in the Welsh village when a huge mountain of coal-mining debris had come rumbling down in an avalanche, engulfing half of the school. On that day 144 people died, 116 of them children aged between seven and ten. The mothers raced to the buried building and dug frantically through the black rubble with their bare hands, searching for their children. They didn't stop even when there was no skin left on their palms.

'She said she wasn't well that day,' the woman said to me, 'but I had to work, so I made her go to school.'

There was the burden that woman had been carrying for decades – she thought she should have listened to her little girl. She felt she'd missed the chance that had been thrown up for her to save her daughter from the horror.

It was hard to explain that she had not killed her daughter. But in the bigger picture that terrible disaster had already begun and all those children were on a timeline leading them to that Friday. That girl's mother didn't begin the Aberfan disaster by sending her daughter to school – she just made an everyday choice that a mother has to make. She might have made the same decision and that day the slag mountain might not have destabilized. Michael might not have got leave for his sister's wedding. The Italian woman might have decided the weather wasn't right for a trip up the World Trade Center.

Maybe everyone has several potential 'endings', as Dronma believes. You come to a junction and you choose one. A little later, there's another choice. You could end up with a maudlin sense of wondering what would have happened if you had taken the other fork and maybe that's when you're meant to be sweeping and say, 'That's how it was meant to be.' Something bigger than you is driving you on. And that's all there is to it.

15

Secrets and Karma

The hardest sittings are the ones where the person who comes to see me carries a burden not just of grief but of anger. When Anne Marie came to see me you could almost see the fury in her. The man who came through from spirit for her was her husband and the process filled me with a feeling of mental exhaustion and of a pressure on my chest. When I asked Anne Marie if her husband had died of a heart attack, she nodded. I understood that he'd been young, only in his late thirties, but the fatigue I sensed was enough to fell any man.

As I struggled to get a clear message from him, Anne Marie started asking me questions. 'Does he know I know?' she demanded.

I was able to tell her that of course he did now and that I understood from him that he was sorry, but she was so furious that I doubted that anything substantial would get through to her. When people are wrapped in a strong emotion like anger they're not receptive to messages from spirit, so it seemed hopeless. The reading became more of a counselling session than an uplifting visit from a loved one.

She told me about her husband. Towards the end of his life they'd had problems in their marriage and he had been working more and more. As a lorry driver, he had been away from her and their two kids for long stretches of time and she had seen how stressed he was and tried to tell him not to take on so much work. They had argued so much that she had begged him to have marital counselling, which had sent him into a fury. When he had collapsed and died she had been devastated, but shortly afterwards she had got another shock.

After the funeral a woman had telephoned her home and, awkwardly, told her that she'd had a house and a three-year-old child with Anne Marie's husband. She lived in Yorkshire, where there was another lorry depot for his company. Her last months with him had also been ruined by rows that had blown up out of nowhere and by his furtive behaviour. When he didn't come home one day she'd called the depot and his workmates had told her about his death in Scotland and about Anne Marie. She had known he was married, but he'd told her that was all over.

Now both women looked back at his behaviour – the workload, the excuses, the discrepancies – and it all fitted together. Not only did they have to endure bereavement and raising children on their own, but they knew they had been betrayed by the person they should have been able to trust the most, and they couldn't ask him why he'd done it. Their happiest memories were undercut by the knowledge that he'd lied to them.

When she came to the sitting with me Anne Marie was nowhere near being able to forgive the man who'd left this devastating legacy. His secret had ruined the lives of two women, and his three children were bound to be affected as well.

Many people take their secrets to the grave. I've had to deliver confessions from the other life on many occasions, which confirm to me that spirits who have passed can't grow and become lighter when they're still burdened with secrets.

When we cross over we see our lives from a much higher perspective, with all our decisions laid out and their consequences clear, and we have to take all that on board. Those in spirit always have help, but for those left behind it can be hard to understand and forgive.

One of my hairdressing clients, a woman called Lisa, asked if I'd give a reading for her father. 'I'm really worried about him,' she told me. 'He's so aggressive now – he bites my mum's head off when she tries to talk to him. He goes out to work every morning in a filthy mood and he's no better when he comes back in the evening. My sister doesn't like going round to see him any more and her kids are really afraid of him. He's their granddad, but it's as though he's turning into a different man. He never used to be like this. Could you give him a reading or a healing? He needs *something*, even if it's just talking to him and trying to get him to tell you what's wrong. He's pushing us all away, but maybe he'd talk to someone outside the family.'

As I knew her dad and he was a very blokey type, not the sort of person to go to a medium, I had to ask Lisa if she thought he'd come and see me voluntarily. I doubted it. I cut his hair and in the last year I'd begun to get wary of him, even before his family had noticed the change in him, because I could all but feel the anger coming off him.

'I'll see him whenever he wants to see me,' I told her. 'Just let me know.'

'We'll leave him for a couple of weeks,' she said, 'and then we'll try and talk him round.'

I thought she was an optimist, but I think she had to be – the dad she loved was cutting himself off from his family without a word of explanation. His bad behaviour was escalating – one day he grabbed hold of her mother and physically shook her, leaving her weeping and wondering what had happened to the man she'd loved for years.

The couple of weeks weren't up when I heard some terrible news – Lisa's father had hanged himself.

As his family tried to come to terms with what had happened, they were contacted by the accountant from his business, who told them that the company had been collapsing for a year or more and that Lisa's father had become increasingly erratic as it had gone on. When he'd left the house in the morning he hadn't gone to his office but to the bookie's to try and win enough money to pay off his debts. He'd also gone to loan sharks to try and prop the firm up, desperate to go on supporting his family. He hadn't breathed a word to his wife or kids and his secret had grown monstrous.

I gave a reading for the family a few months after he took his life, but it was a huge effort. He was a heavy, heavy soul who could barely communicate or offer evidence to his loved ones. His wife sat there bravely and accepted that it just wasn't time for him to clear everything between them yet, but I could tell that both she and her daughters had been left depressed rather than uplifted by what little we'd got. I had to hold up my hands and promise that I'd do another reading. 'You'll know when,' I said. 'Something will change and you'll feel it, or if it strikes me instead I'll call you straightaway.' It was hard to send friends away, but I couldn't give them anything else.

A year or so passed and I saw Lisa again. 'Mum still really wants a sitting,' she insisted. 'I think it's time.' So they all came over to the salon at the end of the day and I tuned into spirit again.

This time the difference was palpable. My spirit guide Chi came through, as he always does when there's been a breakdown in communication but a message needs to reach someone. He helped Lisa's father convey impressions to me.

I felt lighter when I sensed him and that energy registered with his wife and kids in an instant. He told them that he'd killed himself because the pressure had become too much, the loan sharks were threatening his life and his family and he just couldn't take it any more.

He had something positive to bring them. He told his wife he knew she was getting a new house, which she confirmed, as I hadn't known it, and that she was turning a corner in life, moving towards something better. In the aftermath of his suicide his family had been left bewildered, then, as the facts had come out and they had realized the pressure he'd been under, they had understood and begun to forgive. He was grateful for this. He was certain it had helped him clear some of the emotional debt that had weighed him down on the other side.

His own parents and other relatives also came through and passed on messages to let his widow know that they were helping him. He said he knew what he'd done to his family and it was almost as though he'd had to go to spirit to clear his debts.

Sometimes there is no chance to explain a secret before someone passes. I'd just finished a radio interview in San

Francisco when the presenter asked me if I'd see someone she knew who was desperate for some answers.

The following day a lady in her fifties called Maria came to see me at my hotel. Almost immediately I got a sense of a mother coming through, which didn't seem out of the ordinary, but as I told Maria that I thought her mother had died of stomach cancer because I could feel a tenseness and pain in my own stomach, it dawned on me that it wasn't just the illness – the spirit was so anxious that she was tied in knots.

Maria had sat up straighter when I mentioned her mother and I wondered if it was her tension having this effect. She said no, she was nervous but not anxious. It must be the woman in spirit, I realized. I stopped and thought to the spirit, 'Come on, deal with this. Why are you so worried? This is your daughter, isn't it?'

Chi joined us then, to act as go-between, and the communications, which had been bitty and difficult, began to flow. The mother gave names, dates, a town near Boston. It didn't seem to fit in with Maria, as I thought she was from the west coast, but I told her to grab the hotel writing paper from the desk and start making notes, because I knew this was important. A real urgency was replacing the anxiety from spirit, and it was mirrored by Maria, who was nodding as each new piece of evidence was given, clearly rapt.

'I'm so sorry we never got to meet,' was the message that came across, and the next thought she sent me was, 'I know you were looking for me.'

Her daughter smiled and nodded again.

It turned out that Maria's mother, Jenny, had been just 17 years old when she had become pregnant by a young man she barely knew. Her family were strict Presbyterians who were appalled and packed her off to stay with relatives in the town she'd named near Boston so that the neighbours wouldn't find out what had happened. They bulldozed her into having the baby girl adopted by a family they approved of and, when the adoption was complete, coming home to finish school. She became a schoolteacher, partly, I sensed, out of a drive to pay some kind of penance to children, having given up her daughter so easily.

Fifty years later, as she was dying of stomach cancer, she'd had a message from an agency saying her little girl, now grown up, wanted to contact her. She was frightened, not knowing how her daughter would react to her, but she was desperate to see her, so she agreed, but sadly slipped away before Maria could be with her.

She left a bundle of papers and diaries for her to sift through to try to understand who her biological mother was and why she had given her up, but when Maria read through them, she discovered that Jenny had never mentioned her – she hadn't even confided her feelings about her daughter to a personal journal. She felt bitterly let down. How could the woman who had carried her and given birth to her have erased her from her life? Having lost her mother, then found her, then lost her to cancer, then thought she'd learn about her through the diaries, she felt as though she'd lost her a third time.

At the reading, Jenny didn't just give her evidence of her early life, she also tried to explain herself. It was a confession which came through me and Chi with a tremendous rush of nervous energy – it wasn't just that Jenny had wanted to explain herself to her daughter since the moment the agency had contacted her, she'd wanted to do it for 50 years, and yet she'd buried that part of her story so deeply that she'd almost succeeded in closing her mind to it. Maria wept as Jenny said that every time she'd been low or ill, she hadn't had the energy to keep that secret buried and she'd wake in tears, remembering what it had been like to hold her little girl and wondering where she was now and how her life had turned out.

'I lived all my life with this,' she said. 'It never went away. I never wrote about it, but I couldn't let go.'

The most beautiful twist to the sitting was that she told me that Maria's adoptive mother, also called Jenny, was there with her too, helping her clear her spirit. That really blew Maria away. 'That's just what my adoptive mother would do,' she said, and I tried to convey to her the tremendous maternal warmth that I was getting from the second Jenny. The two mothers had a spiritual connection through their daughter and their paths had crossed on the other side. Now both of them were connecting back to their girl.

Jenny had been forced into silence and into denying a part of herself by her parents as a punishment for doing something they had decided was immoral and they had kept control over her long after she had become an adult. Bullies who impose secrecy in this way force their victims into a kind of partnership and isolate them: it's mind control. If that secret is blown wide open, the abuser loses their power, becoming, in the eyes of society, 'that wimp' who beats women, 'that horror' of a parent or 'that pervert' who threatens children. Their nasty secret parallel world is shattered and the victim can break out. I've seen people unburden themselves by telling their story and it's the beginning of the path to recovery – you can see them get lighter as they share it. Sometimes just the act of saying something out loud is enough for the victim to realize for the first time the full extent of what happened to them and to understand that it wasn't their fault.

Sometimes it can seem as though laying a secret bare will cause more problems than it solves, but ultimately that's not true.

A fellow medium called Jane came to see me, wanting to reach her father in spirit. As soon as she walked in I remarked to her that I could sense a horrible negative feeling around her, as though she was encased in something, and she agreed, shaking her head and raising her hands helplessly. She said she'd tried to do the right thing and to be honest, but now she was being attacked for it. She was beginning to lose faith in her own mediumship and was doubting her judgement.

She had been abused as a child by her father's brother and had carried that secret for decades, alone and afraid, not thinking that her parents would believe her if she went to them. Who would have thought that her uncle, whom her father loved, would do something like that to his daughter? She tried in her own way to overcome what had happened, although it made her feel that she was divided from her parents. How could she be close to them if they didn't know about the ordeal she had been through? It was as though they only knew half of her.

In the end, when her father was very ill in hospital, she broke down and told him. It was devastating for her parents to know that they had been unable to protect their child, but they weren't angry with her for keeping the secret. The uncle had long since gone abroad and lost contact with them, something they'd found confusing and hurtful but now understood.

It was Jane's own brother who couldn't cope and who turned on her. He was furious that she had, as he put it, 'burdened' their parents with this, and began shouting at her and cursing her, even having to be removed from his father's bedside in the hospital. He was so verbally abusive to his sister that it almost spilled over into a fight, with him just holding back from throttling her. Why, he spat, hadn't she kept it to herself? Why had she ruined their father's life?

He was so consumed with anger that by the time their father died a while later he had caused a huge amount of damage to the family. At the funeral he again had to be restrained as he swore at his sister, and his mother was caught between her two children just when they should all have been coming together to support one another in grief.

My reading with Jane turned into more of a chat and a counselling session because I could see she wasn't the person that her father needed to reach, even though she blurted out that she was thinking of killing herself because of her brother. He had taken something unthinkable – the abuse she had gone through – and poisoned it even further.

Two weeks later I spoke to her and she was in floods of tears, this time out of sheer relief. Her brother, who was also a Spiritualist, had had a message from his father during a church demonstration. The old man had come through and shamed him thoroughly. 'You have to apologize to your sister, you're breaking her down, and you're killing your mother,' he said via the medium. 'I saw you at my funeral and how you behaved, and if I could have I would have kicked your arse for what you did! Now, you forgive your sister and you help your mother.'

Mortified, the man wept. Every word he'd hurled at Jane flashed through his mind and now he saw how badly he had hurt her and understood how terrible it must have been for her to be trapped by that secret.

Fortunately, when he went to apologize, she was able to forgive him, and together with their mother they were able to begin to stitch the family back together.

We don't have to wait until the end of a life to clear up our secrets and fears. We can act now to stop them driving a wedge between us and the people we love most. We are all individuals, but we're not meant to be isolated. We look for connections in life. To keep that kind of secret is to make yourself an island, to build a fence around yourself that eventually even you cannot see through.

If you do take down that barrier, your life can open up immediately. You can't expect to do anything to your full capacity when you are burning up so much energy in the fear of having your secret uncovered. Think of all the sad, frightened people who could change their lives and lift so much of the darkness out of this world, or even just their own lives, by opening up.

I think of a girl I know who was ill for years, crippled by panic attacks and punishing herself with bulimia. Her mother was torn up with worry, thinking she was dying or had a grave mental illness. One day her daughter finally couldn't stand it any longer and confessed that she was gay. Her mother had no problem with that but the young woman had become convinced that it was wrong and had hugged the knowledge to herself and it had done her great harm. She had cut a huge part of herself away from her family, convinced that they would despise her if they knew, when in fact they were awake all night worrying about her health.

I don't know how many readings I've done where I've had a mother and father sitting opposite me, wanting to reach a son who has killed himself because he was gay and he thought no one would understand. They're left with this numbing, heavy thought weighing down on them: 'If only we had known...' The secret that their child kept meant he could only picture their disappointment and horror, when in fact there was great love and acceptance waiting for him.

I went through something similar as a teenager and young man. I thought I could run away from both the secret of having been abused and the knowledge that I was gay. I was terrified of what people would say to me if they knew. I'd stand around in the pub with a bunch of blokes talking about football and women and being bored out of my mind. I knew very clearly that I was going to live a gay life but I still married because I fell in love with Kate and because I was frightened.

Every time I saw a friend or member of the family I'd have a parallel track of thought running through my head about how they'd hate me if they knew what I was really like. I conjured up all those 'opinions' without ever knowing what they actually thought. I felt I was a different person from the one they knew. That's where the fear that something terrible was about to happen to my family came from. It ran over into other areas of my life – when we had a holiday to Disneyland I worried that the plane would crash and when we landed safely of course I thought the kids would be killed on a ride while I was just standing there watching. Business decisions were nearly impossible for me because I didn't trust my own judgement – if I was both this gay person and the man who was committed to his wife, how could I know who I was or what I thought? For every thought I had, there was another to contradict it. I thought being gay was destroying me, but it wasn't, it was the secrecy.

Much of my life – 11 years – was dedicated to the marriage and to trying to 'overcome' a fundamental part of myself, a ridiculous effort. It was like trying to change the colour of my skin or the way my hair grew out of my head. All this time I had niggly little health problems like stomach cramps and terrible headaches that I thought were migraines but weren't. I didn't cheat on Kate or try to lead a double life, although there are plenty of marriages out there were one partner sneaks around behind the other's back. Their guilt turns the secret into something shameful and embarrassing, which only escalates their sense of themselves as a 'bad person'.

Finally the moment came when I realized that I hadn't done anything wrong and that at the core of all these fears was the simple fact that I wasn't straight. That was all.

You can sit under a cloud of fear, not realizing your potential, until you die. I can just picture what I would have been like now if I hadn't come out – a man in his forties, still worrying if his kids went out anywhere, still thinking there was something deeply wrong with him and that everyone was just waiting to attack him.

You could spend a lifetime desperately fleeing your real self, only to find yourself in a dark underworld of your own making. I should know – I nearly did it. But when you come clean both to yourself and to others, there can be a moment of huge relief and then a clear perspective on the very things that tied you in knots before. With the luxury of hindsight you can marvel at all the horrific scenarios that you let go through your mind and the energy you spent on them, and reflect that if they didn't happen then, they probably won't now. Perhaps you can take a new direction in life, one that's true to the real you.

In my case, my worst fear did actually happen. Years after I'd split with Kate and when I'd been with Jim for some time, I still hadn't let on to most of the people around me that we were living together. My sons knew, as did Kate, my sisters and parents, but Jim and I had this hilarious idea that no one had noticed that we were a couple.

'So are you and Jim together, then?' a friend would ask and I'd say, 'Oh, noooo.' And then of course Jim and I would leave the Spiritualist meetings together and drive home in the same car. Everyone must have been splitting their sides with laughter at that. Even Jim's mother, whom he hadn't told he was gay, left some money to me in her will. Every time he went round for tea she'd say, 'How is Gordon?' and he'd look at his feet and mutter, 'Oh, I haven't seen him for ages.' It was perfectly obvious to everyone and yet there we were, sneaking around.

One day Katie rang me and said, 'I've just spoken to someone from the *News of the World*. They want to run a story about you living with Jim.'

That sort of thing had been a recurring nightmare for me. Imagine everyone learning about your secret in the paper! There would be some horrible snatched shot of you trying to hide your face and then an exposé about your love life and your friends would never talk to you again.

What a ridiculous situation we'd set up for ourselves. Instead of coming out we were being flung out and it never would have happened if we'd been truthful. That was the mad thing – it was all self-inflicted. We'd pretended not to live our actual life and look what had happened. It was a real karmic slap in the face!

I sat down and did a practice I'd done in a development class years ago, where you ask yourself what your fear is and then walk straight into it. Then I phoned the *News of the World* and invited them to come and interview me and Jim at home. The journalists had been told a bunch of lies about the whole saga, so we set the record straight and posed for cheesy photos. Running head-first into that fear turned out to be the biggest commitment we could have made to each other. It still holds.

Afterwards I phoned my dad, still rattling with nerves, and let him know what to expect, and he just said, 'First of all, son, I don't read the *News of the World*, and secondly are your boys OK with this? Have you fixed that?' I told them that both my sons had said they were fine with it. 'OK,' he went on, 'is there anything else you need to say?'

'No...'

'You're my son and I love you.'

And that was the end of the conversation and it was perfect.

When the article came out we were braced for the phone to start ringing, but it turned out that people couldn't care less! They just thought we were daft for letting it become such a source of worry. That was a great lesson – all that terror about how I was going to be judged and what it would do to my friendships, and it turned out that it just didn't matter to most people. There's often a very egotistical side to some secrets, of thinking that you're the object of everyone's fascination and that the scandal will blow them all away, but it might turn out that you might make a few seconds' chat over a cup of tea and then they're on to the next subject.

I've grown to hate secrets. They usually spell trouble. You have to shine a light into those shadows, not be policed by fear. Go into your mind and open all the doors. Ask yourself, 'What's holding me here?' Whatever it is, you have to accept it as soon as you can, not bury it under a stone or it will crush you. Talk about it, be real, accept it as part of you.

Hiding the truth escalates bad karma; it takes you along a difficult path. You cannot live your life if you are not open and free. If you are your own person, you'll be happier and more compassionate to those around you. If you go against your natural instincts, you'll put yourself through hell.

My philosophy is to open up as much as you can in every direction of your life. I've tried being secretive and it was physically exhausting, as well as taking its mental toll. It drove a wedge between me and my loved ones. It wasn't fair to them. As you open up, you connect to everyone and everything.

I can tell when someone is trying to conceal something. I know the signs – and it's nothing to do with being psychic. If you know someone who's obviously labouring under a secret, try to be patient and let them open up in their own time. Be gentle. You have to be patient with yourself too. It can take a lifetime to get to know yourself and to face all those secrets and fears. Maybe an incident from your past suddenly surfaces in your memory, making you pay attention to something that you tried to push away before because you just weren't ready to take on board what it meant. Perhaps someone hurt you but for now you want to excuse what they did, not think about the consequences for you over the years. Sometime it'll click and you'll be able to piece it all together.

Unravelling yourself is a lifetime's work and sometimes it takes a huge life event before you realize something about yourself that you came to this world to understand. But the whole idea of karma is to get to the point, to find the truth and to gain understanding.

16

'Are We Here to Learn a Specific Lesson?'

At some point in spirit, before you came into this life, your consciousness chose what would happen to it in this world. Often, we've chosen huge hardships and trials – a serious disease or a disability, a premature death or a loss. That might mean heartbreak, the loss of someone close to us, being part of some horrifying historical event or anything that takes an emotional toll above the ordinary on us.

We lose that plan when we come into the world, along with our strong awareness of spirit, which we have to find again as we progress through life. There is a reason for this. If at 12 you remembered that you were going to die a violent death at 35, what kind of existence would you have? If we do get a glimpse of the blueprint ahead of us, whether through a communication from spirit or in some other way, the point of it is to prove to us that there is a bigger plan out there, not to reveal our entire life story.

But why would you choose to take on something like a serious illness? Why would you plan something that would break your husband's heart or plunge your mother into grief?

I always remember trying to reassure a woman who'd lost her son in a work accident. She believed in predestination, but it was hard for her to come to terms with the idea that her son had chosen to die at only 28 and devastate her. Every life has to have an ending and he had had a very full 28 years before then. But what could she hope to take as consolation for that one second when he died?

The answer lies in the potential for good that can come as a result of a big karmic event like that. It's in the aftermath of a death, not the death itself, that the biggest lessons are learned and the greatest amounts of darkness are burned away.

Whether you are the direct victim or the collateral damage – like Sonia, who lost her son – your harsh experiences have a force to them. You burn up bad karma when you take them on and battle through them and grow. That's why we give ourselves those opportunities.

Even a horrendous murder can help those left behind to make sense of the senseless. The people who suffer most in this life are not victims of a curse, and no great being is punishing them, they are just the most spiritually brave people among us, the ones who take on a karmic payload that would overwhelm many. They show the rest of us how to handle it all. Those severe experiences can make them richer by far: I've known people who have accepted horrendous loss in their lives and have realized that they still had to live on despite that. The loss became positive spiritual energy because they knew that they had been tested to the limit and that no one on Earth could hurt them so badly again.

As individuals we're all at different levels of spiritual growth. Some come into this world to learn the simplest lessons, others to take on daunting amounts of karma. It's selfless and brave to throw yourself into the battle. And even the briefest lives can teach us a lot about life and living.

One of the hardest twists of fate to take can be the loss of a child during a pregnancy or at birth. The lifespan is so short that there seems to be no clue as to why that child needed to come into your life and then to leave it. What was the purpose behind it all? People always want to know if that baby will be connected to them, because they feel that never having held a living child they haven't had time to bond. But they felt that child within them, or knew about it, and nobody but them has had that particular experience. You don't need a scan to know that.

A hairdresser I knew once asked me to give a reading for a friend who'd suffered a loss, and I agreed without knowing what to expect. Debbie was a nice-looking woman, with blonde curls and an open, friendly face. The message that came through for her was a strange one for me, because normally I expect to hear from a specific spirit but instead I saw three cherubs, two boys and a little girl, hovering around her. That was all I saw.

That friendly face dissolved into tears and Debbie said, 'Those are my babies, aren't they?'

'What do you mean?' I asked.

She explained that she'd had three miscarriages and although they were all early in the pregnancy, she'd felt sure that two had been boys and the third a girl. She thought of them as her little angels and that's exactly how they appeared to me, as these sweet mythical beings keeping her company. What I saw and told her became the perfect confirmation to her that her instincts had been right all along.

Very often I tell people that spirit will give us exactly what we need, whether it's to heal, like Debbie, or to receive comfort because we're about to face a terrible trial. Debbie had her little angels and knew they could come to her and that no matter what, they were still connected to her. Love had already begun to form its bond.

The very fact that you can have a sense of loving an unborn child, or a child that only lives a short time, is in itself a very pure, strong thing. All that child ever knew was a sense of love and connection. It did not have to go through any of the hardships of this existence and yet it changed its parents' lives forever.

A child's death becomes an experience that the parents have to go through together or apart. I know several couples whose relationship has been strengthened by grief. Fathers in particular find themselves having to open up and grow in order to support their partner and break away from the stereotype of the strong and silent but emotionally numb man.

A death can open up a deep reserve of strength and spiritual awareness that is more powerful than grief. That's the stuff that changes lives, communities and even the world.

When Margaret Mizen's son Jimmy was brutally murdered in a bakery in south-east London in 2008 she spoke of forgiveness: 'People keep saying, "Why aren't you angry?" There's so much anger in this world and it's anger that's killed my son. If I am angry, then I am exactly the same as this man. We have got to get rid of this anger, we have just got to.'

You could see she was gutted and that she was still reeling from the heaviest blow imaginable, but she stood there and talked of two lives – of her son and his killer. She'd grasped the essential truth that the human species is not very spiritually evolved and that we will go on inflicting pain on one another until we wake up and see the consequences of our actions.

These premature deaths aren't a punishment, they're a sign that we are making no progress on this Earth and are also a superhuman effort to remove some of that darkness from our collective karma. As long as there are lessons to be learned, these things will happen.

Forgiveness is the precious jewel in emotional and spiritual growth: forgiveness of ourselves and of others. Learning to forgive for the sake of peace will lead to peace, for all concerned. The victim who can truly forgive from the very depths of themselves is much more powerful than any force that ever threatened them.

Looking around at the world today you can see examples of both our spiritual development and the ways in which we're trapped in ignorance and lack of compassion. It's only a few decades since, for example, whole towns in America were segregated to keep black and white people apart, but now it's unthinkable that the government would uphold such laws. But you could also pick any one of the wars playing out now and see people treating other people as though they were lower than animals.

As an individual you can't change the world's karma single-handedly, but you can make your contribution by finding reserves of strength within yourself and building a compassion that transforms yourself and others. As we evolve we take on more experiences and grow, picking more difficult destinies as we become more aware, until we're in a state where our human consciousness is very close to that of spirit.

The experiences of loss and suffering in this life force us to realize how one action or one death can bring pain to others – pain we have experienced ourselves – until we find ourselves unable to meet hatred and ignorance with more hatred and ignorance.

Every life is important, long or short, adventurous or dull, and every life can be a lesson to others. We can all take great spiritual steps forward. We can reap good karma from the tiniest actions in our lives and it will contribute to the greater good karma of the human race.

17

'Can We Overcome Trauma in This Lifetime?'

I remember an Irishwoman who came to me for a reading. She was somewhere in her forties and very thin, with huge, worried eyes and high cheekbones. Her hair was pulled back tightly from her face. I got the sense of a baby's presence, a child that she had lost, and told her so. I added that she would always have a connection to that child and that I got the impression from it that she should forgive herself. She wiped her eyes and kept her lips pursed. When the reading was over she chatted to me and then slowly told me her story.

She'd been married to a violent, bullying man whom she had grown to hate. They already had several children when she realized that she was pregnant again, and because she was terrified of her husband's reaction to the news, she arranged to go to England to have an abortion. She didn't want to bring another child into a house that was already filled with fear of this man and she knew she couldn't leave him until their children were grown. So she lied and said she was popping over to stay with a friend in London.

Her husband had such a grip on her mind that when she got back from her secret trip she wasn't able to tell him what she'd done, because she thought he would kill her. Every time she brought up a similar subject she said he'd 'go nuts'. She didn't dare tell any of her friends either, in case word got back to her husband, and she was also wracked with guilt. She thought she'd sent the baby to purgatory, and then she tried to convince herself that it had never had consciousness and its life hadn't begun, but she was torn by the thought of this lost child. Should she have carried on with the pregnancy, even if her husband beat her? Would it have been cruel to bring a child into the world saddled with that man as a father?

For years she carried that stone around in her heart, grieving on her own with no support, cutting herself off from everyone around her, and then, when her children had grown up, she finally left her husband and moved to England to start a new life. For the first time she found friends in whom she was able to confide and they tried to reassure her that she'd done the right thing, but still she went on with this sickness in her soul and the conviction that she was in hell. Even with the Irish Sea between her and her husband she was scared that he would kill her if he knew about it.

By hearing from the child and knowing that it was OK, she found some peace. I felt that she knew she was on a bigger journey and she'd come to the reading to collect that acknowledgement from the child whom she had protected from an abusive man. She was also having to mend fences with her other children, whose childhood had been darkened by the shadow of their violent father.

To me, the great lesson that she'd chosen before she came into this life wasn't suffering the loss of her child but dealing with her husband. It must have been apparent from early on in the relationship that he was a bully, but out of fear she made a series of decisions to stay with him, culminating in the choice to have an abortion. And yet the psychological load she carried only grew heavier the longer she stayed with him. Now she was working hard to mend the damage done.

She told me that when she finally left him she'd had to spend six months in a women's refuge in order to qualify for accommodation of her own and that she'd seen young girls in their teens there, with babies on their laps, who'd already had the courage to escape abusive relationships.

She couldn't believe their bravery and looked back at the 20 years she'd spent with her husband with even more regret.

In karmic terms, she'd taken on far more than those girls, but I knew that she would never let herself get into the same situation again, in this life or a future existence. Her husband had to learn, too, but I suspected that he didn't have the insight or the humility to see that what he had done was wrong – his spirit will take far longer to understand his life and actions.

You might say that woman had 'ruined her life', but it couldn't be further from the truth – she'd taken on that big karmic payload and taken bad decisions, then fought to overcome them when she realized she wasn't as weak as she'd thought. I'd see her as a heroine and an example to others.

Occasionally I give a reading for someone who has had a loved one taken from them in a way that's so awful that I struggle to understand how anyone could pick themselves up afterwards and go on. When I first met Jackie Clarkson, an Englishwoman who lives in South Africa, I was struck by what a lovely, bubbly lady she was, but when I met her for a private reading and afterwards learned what had happened, I was just filled with admiration. I think you'll understand when you read her story in her own words:

I first saw Gordon on The Noeleen Show *and I thought that if I saw anyone about my daughter, it would be him because I thought I could relate to him. When my husband heard he was coming to South Africa again he booked tickets to go and see him. There were a lot of people in the audience but at one point Gordon singled out my husband and said, 'You light a candle every night,' which was true – my husband has lit a candle every night since our daughter died. It wasn't my daughter who was communicating through Gordon, though, but her husband, Daryl, who thanked my husband for his gesture. He gave some other pieces of evidence about his love of sports cars (he was doing up an old stock car for racing at the time of his death).*

I work for British Airways and the next day I was at my job when I spotted Gordon in the departure lounge and went over for a chat. He said he'd arrange a private reading when he was next in South Africa.

On his next trip, a friend who'd also lost a daughter and I went to see him at his hotel. It was all very informal. He sat on the bed and I pulled up a chair. I didn't say much, but he took my hand and the first thing he said was, 'There's a Romeo and Juliet here,' and I knew it was Melissa and Daryl.

I couldn't believe how calm I was throughout the reading. I got the impression that Gordon saw a lot more than he would have liked to relate to me, and he said, 'You've been through absolute hell.'

This time there were messages from Melissa. She said I had a framed photo by my bed and that morning before I'd left I'd kissed it. I think possibly Gordon saw how broken down I could have been, but every time I'm down something happens to guide me in the right direction. I've got a sense of humour still and I know Melissa wouldn't have wanted me to give up. Every time I think about what happened to her, I get a sense of calmness coming over me, and it's as if Melissa is telling me it's not important.

That's just what she was like in life – she was always protecting me, always looking out for me and I think she's still there egging me on. It might sound strange to say this, but I think I'm fortunate because I know when it's my time to go I'm going to have her there to welcome me.

She was a beautiful girl. She looked like a model. She was what you'd call an old soul. People used to be surprised at how young she was, which bothered her, but it was because of her demeanour, not that she looked older. She never gave me an ounce of trouble from the moment she was born. She met Daryl, who was a few years older than her and they had a beautiful wedding, with a horse-drawn carriage bringing her to the chapel, all the works. People came from all over the world to be there.

They'd only been married a year when they were killed. The man who led the gang, Vincent, worked for Daryl, and he'd even been at the wedding. His father had worked for Daryl's father. They came to Melissa's house because they thought that Daryl would have lots of money in the safe.

*Melissa was at home because her new dog had just been
spayed and she was looking after it. They held Daryl and
Melissa hostage and tied them to chairs, and when they
realized that there wasn't anything to steal they made them
phone up Daryl's parents, Frans and Gina, and tell them to
come over for a barbecue or something. And then of course
they attacked them as well.*

*They kept them prisoner in that house from nine o'clock
in the morning to about eleven o'clock at night. It all got
out of hand because the gang started drinking. I only found
out much later that they forced rat poison in coffee on them.
Melissa didn't drink coffee and the police told me they found
it splattered everywhere, so she must have thrown it.*

*I actually phoned her that morning, while it was all
going on. I asked what she was up to and she said she was
out shopping with Daryl, and I asked, 'Are you all right?'
and she said, 'Mummy, I'm fine.' She never called me
'Mummy', she only called me 'Mum'. Then the phone went
dead and I thought, 'Oh blimey, she doesn't want me there.'
I thought she might have been having a tiff with her husband
and that I shouldn't phone back because I didn't want to
be an interfering mother-in-law. Imagine how I've tortured
myself over that. They must have had a gun to her head.
Why did they let her answer the phone? Was she protecting
me? And where did she find the strength?*

*I didn't find out for a while after it happened that they'd
raped both her and Gina. Late at night they drove them out
into the veldt – can you imagine that drive? It was a two-*

hour journey. And then they shot them all. Gina got free and
they kicked her down a ravine.

My husband and I were at the airport when we found out
and he just kept saying, 'Were they all together?' At least
they had that.

The police caught Vincent and the others. When we went
to court his grandparents were there and they were horrified.
The district attorney said he'd never tried a case as bad; he
broke down and sobbed his heart out afterwards. Vincent
was only in prison for a few weeks when he was killed – he
was 22, just two years younger than Melissa. I would have
liked to have visited him and asked him why he did it. If
you want money, why don't you rob a bank? Why go to
someone's house to do it?

I also feel quite strongly that Melissa had some kind of
premonition of what was going to happen. There was a case
where a girl called Alison was travelling to Port Elizabeth
when she was attacked and raped by two guys. They slit
her throat and slashed her stomach open, but somehow she
survived. I'd seen Melissa reading a book she had written
about her experiences, called I Have Life, and it seemed
odd that she was so drawn to that case, as she wasn't a big
reader.

I still don't know half of what went on and it's been five
years now. It's taken this long to come to terms with the fact
that Melissa's not here any more. I still think she could walk
through the door.

Sometimes I feel better when I talk about it; I don't want

Melissa, Daryl, Frans and Gina to be forgotten, but people don't want to bring them up in conversation because it was so horrible.

I would like to think that when she went through all that she had some inner strength. I do think she's very strong now and she's there helping us in her own subtle way.

Two days after she died there was a moment when I felt that my whole body was warm, as if somebody was hugging me, really physically putting their arms around me, and I haven't felt that since. I don't dream about her much but when I do it's never a nightmare. In one dream she was laughing and happy, dressed in a long blue velvet gown with her long hair curled and loose.

I know we all love our kids, but she was definitely my soul mate. We spoke every single day. You know as a mother you bring up your children, do the best by them and you just protect, protect, protect, and when somebody comes and violates them like that it's unbearable.

People say you've got lessons to learn and I'm a lot more compassionate now than I used to be. I listen to people's problems more. My son says he can't believe that I'm not lecturing him about his life and he loves me for it. All I want is to love him and for him to be safe and happy. I don't care about anything else. It's what I've learned from Melissa – I don't have to go screeching through life getting all my ducks in a row.

I have to do more for myself now. I know that if I go down, everyone else will too. My friends here in South Africa *have got me through. They're my support system, along with my husband, who's become a very spiritual person. I think he's made his peace and worked it all out, with Melissa's help.*

The way that Jackie spoke of Melissa's inner strength reminded me of a sitting I did in Boston, where an elderly woman who had been raped and murdered in her own home came through to reassure her grieving granddaughter, telling her that her attacker had never touched her soul. She said her experience would bring light to others, which seemed impossible to me – how could good come of that awful crime? – but now I understand better. The bright light of spirit is not affected by human defilement. I'm sure Melissa drew on spirit, too, and it's clear to me that she's become her mother's guardian angel now.

Melissa was innocently caught up in a kind of national karma of hatred between black and white South Africans which is a legacy of apartheid and the colonial system. It's a violent, troubled karma which won't be cleared until enough people wake up to what's going on and change the way they think. Her death was in the psyche of the country and nothing her mother could have done would have saved her. Her family will have to reconcile themselves to the knowledge that this atrocity was part of a greater problem. Their fight is against ignorance and unthinking violence. They will win, with Melissa's help, by not losing their own humanity. Jackie's warmth and character, and the way she has bravely gone on with her life, gave me hope for them.

18

'What Are You Afraid of?'

Back when I was learning to develop as a medium in Glasgow there was regular group of us who'd meet to practise meditation and talk things through. Because of the way we had to examine our lives and bare our souls together, we became quite a strong group of friends and we kept in touch during the rest of the week.

One of my friends from the group used to call for a chat quite often and it seemed that she always had a new worry. 'Did you see that on the news?' she'd say, about something horrendous that had happened in another city or at the other end of the country. 'Can you imagine? What if my kids had been caught up in it? I haven't slept. Just think about it.' Sometimes these disasters even took place in another country, but she'd still ring up and fret about them happening to her loved ones, and she really made herself hugely depressed picturing her children going through all kinds of horrific experiences – car crashes, school shootings, earthquakes, you name it.

I told her she should get rid of her telly and stop reading the news, but really it was hard to see someone living in such a horrible state of fear, and all of it self-inflicted. In the end I'd had enough and said, 'You're a kind person, but you need to recognize the difference between empathy and compassion. What good are you doing by imagining your kids in a situation that's nothing to do with them? What good are you going to do for the people who are actually suffering?'

All this emotional energy was just burning up into nothing, but she wasn't foolish and after a while she took stock of what she was doing and found something better to do with herself. She volunteered for ChildLine on a regular basis and found she could actually make a difference. The empathy was transformed into compassion when she started to really listen honestly to people and understand the depth of their problems. It goes without saying that she was actively helping people and even helping change lives – it certainly changed hers.

One of the most important things about this was that at the end of her shift she could simply walk away, knowing that she had done her bit. She didn't need to ring me up and tell me that she'd had some awful calls that evening and the world was a terrible place, because she knew it wasn't her baggage.

It's hard to look at the world today, when every news bulletin seems to bring more bad news, and not want to just throw up your hands, buy lots of tinned food and shut your kids up in the house for the rest of their lives so they're safe. As another war breaks out or another child is abducted, you could be forgiven for thinking that humanity is doomed and the Earth plane is nothing but evil and that if you're not constantly on your guard those dark forces could come for you and your loved ones.

I think it's child abductions that prey the most on people's minds. Whenever a child disappears everyone worries about that poor kid and then takes that worry into their own lives. They think, 'I left my kid in the garden, what if she'd been taken too?' Suddenly you're a better person because you won't let your kids play outside, and they're all safe at home with the PlayStation and some nice children from across the street who get driven over by their mother in a 4x4 with bull bars – forgetting that they're both more likely to be killed in a traffic accident than abducted and murdered! Pretty soon you're looking at everyone who walks past your gate with suspicious eyes. A great horror looms over your life, the idea that you will make some small slip and bang, your child will be gone and you will spend the rest of your life torturing yourself with regret.

Yet there must be a billion kids running around the planet and most of them aren't getting abducted. Many of them *are* dying because they only have filthy water to drink or live in shanty towns like the ones I saw in Soweto. But we seem to have lost perspective. How did we come to have such a strange idea of the dangers of life?

When I was a kid we all played out in the streets all day. Our mums would chuck us out after breakfast and that was that. They knew that other people in the neighbourhood would keep an eye on us and make sure we weren't doing anything too risky, but other than that we were left to our own devices. It wasn't that they didn't love us, it was that they weren't afraid. Love and lack of fear aren't mutually exclusive.

Nowadays, like my friend in the development circle who worried about things that never happened to her family, we often confuse empathy and compassion and make our own hell. When we do this, a huge reservoir of negative feeling builds up and nothing positive actually comes of it. A few individuals will do something like setting up a support group for victims or trying to have a new piece of legislation passed to prevent future crimes, but what about the rest of us?

If you are forever worrying about what might happen or are badly affected by something that's happened to a stranger, you need space where you can sit down and ask yourself why. The aftermath of the death of Princess

Diana was strange to me. I had to wonder what was going on in the country when so many people were weeping as though they'd lost someone in their own family. It's partly due to the way that news is reported around the world simultaneously, so we think we are feeling emotions collectively and that what's touching people we have never met is also affecting us. But if you feel overwhelming sadness at a stranger's death there might be a sadness in your own life which needs to be addressed. You need to face something that's been left unresolved and to accept it and move on. Then, once you're settled in yourself, you can really begin to make a difference to others.

Power is also generated when people pray together or work for change. After Dunblane there was a universal prayer around the world and there was a real strength to it – we weren't the only nation to have suffered something like that atrocity, and the acknowledgement of that made a fellow feeling. When horrors like the tsunami or Dunblane or Locherbie befall others, even if we don't know them personally, the connection between human spirits becomes stronger. The world stops for a minute and we ask bigger questions and begin to wonder if we should expect more spiritually from our lives.

OK, you might be saying, but not everything is in our control and bad things do happen, and even if the odds are small, they might still happen to me or a loved one. My working in a charity shop or being spiritually aware won't prevent my car from being hit by a drunk driver or my child from being in the wrong place at the wrong time. That's true, but if you want to do your bit to protect your loved ones, the best thing you can do is not contribute to the darkness in the world. Take action to improve things when you can. Feel your emotions but don't invent them – have they been whipped up by a newspaper or have they come from your heart? Ask a few questions about the things you read and ask more questions of yourself. Stay grounded and reach out to help others when you are able and willing.

For me, the turning point in anyone's life comes when they realize just how many of the things they were afraid of never happened. Not everything you think of will happen, and you have to realize that. Thought is not real life.

If you let your thoughts run away with you, you can allow fear to come into you and fill you up until you can barely breathe, but then you can barely live either, and if something terrible does happen, what good will it do you to say, 'I knew that would happen'? What difference will it make? None at all.

What we need is to turn fear to our advantage. Fear can be the emotion that forces us to look to ourselves for answers and to move away from something harmful. Often it causes a person to look for answers from a much higher force than themselves and explore spirit for the first time. If you can transform the energy of fear into energy for action, who knows what you can achieve?

Daily meditation is a great way to step back from that overload of information and feelings, take on board what you need and let the rest float away. Some people do that by writing a diary, which is also very effective.

You may find that with regular meditation you sleep much better and dream less. I haven't dreamed much in the 15 years I've been meditating. I think that's because the meditation allows me to get beyond the dream stage and into much deeper sleep. I find that if I've overdone things, though, I'll end up dreaming my day: a mishmash of everything that happened runs through my head and in the morning I wake up feeling good, as though someone got all the paperwork off my mental desk and organized it.

When your mind is filled with sorrow, in chaos or consumed by rage it will cause suffering in your inner self. What is lacking is understanding. To reach that you must first learn to quieten your mind and cut yourself off from distractions from the outside world. Find a quiet place where you can relax, a place where you feel comfortable and know that you will not be disturbed, and try this meditation.

A Meditation for Relaxation

Take control of your breathing. Breathe in through your nose, deep into your lungs. Release the breath slowly from your body. You are now gaining control of your body and mind. You are not being trapped by emotional thoughts or fears.

With each in-breath tell yourself to relax and with each out-breath tell yourself to release. It's a direct command from your mind to relax your body and release any tensions.

If any thoughts enter your mind, just let them pass through. Recognize that they are just thoughts and let them go. Focus only on your breathing and relaxing and releasing.

You are now creating harmony between body and mind. You are fortifying your mind and taking charge of any thoughts you allow there. You are also creating space for peace to fill your heart.

Be at peace. Mind and body are as one.

19

Swimming in the Karmic Soup

One way to have total control of your karma is to withdraw from the world like a guru and sit in a cave and meditate all day. Obviously that's not really an option for most of us! We have to plunge into life and find ourselves on timelines whose endings we can't guess, bracing ourselves for the worst and hoping for the best.

It might help to believe that there are two levels of karma – that karmic soup of little actions that can lead to big consequences in which we swim every day and a bigger force that can override our choices. That's the karma that's at national level or even that of the human race itself.

We spend our lives swimming in this karmic soup: thick, heavy emotions that just lie there and never dissipate. We walk around in them all day, not seeing them, even when they're dragging us down like a kind of emotional gravity. Everything we see, read or hear affects us: a disaster in a foreign country, a kidnapping, an accident. We see these things on the telly and go to sleep with a head full of them. We're afraid that something bad will happen to us or to our loved ones, or perhaps we're bowed down with something from our past that we haven't dealt with and it's blanketing our life now. We fill our brains with information that's all negative and that we make no effort to process, and our inner voice gets pushed aside.

Often we don't want to wake up and be in the world because we think we can't cope with it. Some folk drink or take drugs to escape. Others just go into what I call the 'dream stream', where they are walking about, going about their business and their lives without being able to honestly look at them and say, 'Yes, I want this and it's a good thing.' In this state we can take decisions that change our future without really thinking about them and knowing our real feelings. Years later we wake up and wonder how we got to a place where we never wanted to be, but it was nothing to do with bad luck or circumstances – we were sleepwalking.

It's possible to live in this world and know that there will be huge highs and lows and that we're all swept along by something bigger, while still having some control and hope. It's all about learning lessons, not being dragged blindly through great suffering. We can get great soul understanding from many different experiences, both good and bad. Look to the joyful, the ecstatic times too – there are lessons to learn there as well.

If you can accept that a lot of the worst things that happen in life are a way of burning up karma, you can begin to put a positive spin on your life. You have the choice to turn the difficult things into a punishment or a life lesson.

Some people can take these things calmly. I remember as a kid going round to a friend's house to see if he'd come out to play and his mum answered the door and said gently that he couldn't come out as his father had just died. Her husband had passed very suddenly, sitting in his chair in the living room. She'd gone in to take him a cup of tea and there he was. I was shocked and ran to my mum to tell her, and the next thing we saw the woman calmly going to the shops to get something. We all thought she was just in shock and she'd crack up later – people in my street tended to be a bit more dramatic about this kind of thing! – but she never did. Her husband had nearly died in a serious accident a few years earlier and she must have had time to face the possibility of his death then. When it came, she was mentally prepared.

I'm not saying you have to suppress your real feelings. If you let all the little things build up, all the stuff you swallowed and let get under your skin, one day a bigger incident will be the lightning rod for all those emotions and bang, you'll be unable to cope because you've got three years' worth of pent-up feelings to deal with at once.

Chi once explained some aspects of our minds and emotions to a group of us in a trance session. He told us to think of our minds as having three levels: 'waking consciousness', which is the immediate, thinking part of our brains, 'emotional', the place in which we feel our experiences, and 'repressed', where we try to bury trouble and trauma. We have to clear that upper, intelligent part of the mind and keep it calm and uncluttered in order to let our emotions rise to that thinking place and be understood for what they are and where they really come from. If problems sink to the lowest level and are suppressed, lying like stones in the very pit of our psyche, they can cause us huge fear and uncertainty. If we don't try to dredge them up and understand them, they will lead to phobias and depression.

So use your thinking mind to go to where your feelings can be found. That way you can recognize them and deal with them. Visualizing this as going into different rooms will give you direction and help you to go within.

A Meditation for Past Problems

In meditation walk towards a house. Walk slowly but confidently towards the front door.

Open the door and go and stand in the centre of the circular hall. See that there are seven doors around the hall. Each room represents an important phase of your life development. (You can divide this into seven-year cycles, as I choose to, or any other way that fits your experience.)

Enter one of the rooms. It may symbolize a time of your life that you want to look at or one where you know there is a significant event that you haven't dealt with.

If it is dark, switch on the light. Open curtains, let in as much light as you can.

See yourself as you were at that time. Spend time examining any episodes that affected you greatly. Take yourself back to any emotional places where you felt helpless, sad or defeated. Recognize that you may have done things that you were not proud of or have been terrified and in need of rescue. Ask yourself, 'What can I do to help that person? How would I encourage them not to feel bad about themselves?'

Hold the child or person and heal them. You have the strength to make them feel safe and secure.

Leave the room, knowing that you have brought compassion to the person you once were and created light in those episodes of your life.

Love yourself for who you have become and congratulate yourself on who you are about to become. You are going to become a more compassionate person than you were in the past. You can understand and forgive now, with wisdom, because you can let go and grow and not be trapped as that frightened individual was.

You can return to go into the other rooms whenever you feel able.

Shining a light into your own mind can take away any darkness.

20

The Power of Prayer

A woman once asked me if I could do some kind of special prayer to spirit to make her son's girlfriend lose their baby. You can imagine the response she got! I don't know where she got the idea that she could bring down a horrible curse on someone dear to her own son, but it can't have been from a sermon in a Spiritualist church. Similarly, I once had a woman who considered herself a very devout Catholic ask if she could pray *her* son's partner away. I don't think so!

What if she'd got her wish? What new timeline might her son have ended up on? What might he have gone through? I don't think she'd bothered to realize what she was really asking for. She needed to take a good long look at her own feelings to see where that hatred came from.

Prayer at its best is something you do when you care for someone – be it a relative, a friend or a stranger whose story you saw on the news – and ask for your good wishes to them to be amplified by a divine source. It's also a request for strength and for clarity, so that you can hold yourself together through tough times and understand in an objective way what's happening, rather than be swept along by rising emotions.

What prayer is not about is pushing away your responsibility or rehashing your fears in a monologue with God. I used to pray for all the bad things to go away, but that was just a fear of experience and life. Don't *pray* for your child to behave better – talk to him, or get help. Don't talk to God about your husband's drinking – talk to him, or an expert counsellor. Then pray for the ability to deal with it all. That Catholic lady needed to stop complaining to God about her son's girlfriend and to talk to her son and the girl instead. Don't beg God and the universe for things when there's so much that is within your own power to change, including your attitude to life and to those around you.

Prayer tends not to deliver obvious results instantly – a big hand won't come down from the sky and give you that man you were hoping for. But one prayer is enough – you can assume it was heard the first time.

Effie Ritchie used to pray for everyone in the world. She'd start with her family and friends and then she'd move on to 'that woman I saw today who looked awful poor,' and all the kids in the hospital, and the nurses who looked after them, and the doctors, and on she'd go till three in the morning.

'What the hell was I doing?' she asked me once when she remembered her spiritual overdrive. 'I didn't need to do all that. In the end I just said, "God, you know how to handle this better than I do, you look after them, I can't stay up all night."'

She taught me that the best thing was a concentrated, thoughtful prayer, and as a fantastic healer, she also knew it was more important to heal one person well than to try and sort the whole world out. That way you cleared what you could of the darkness and did your bit.

21

Turning Points

Lots of books tell you how to make 'affirmations' and say, 'I'm beautiful' or 'I am a good person.' It's good to send these messages to yourself as a pick-me-up and they can shape not only your day but also your attitude to life, but a lot of these advice tomes go further and take affirmations into the realm of hopes and dreams. 'I am going to be rich today,' they advise you to say, or, 'I will find a fiancé by the end of this year,' and that's where I part company with the authors.

We've already seen that a lot of the things we dream of come as a result of concrete choices made in the present, not just because they were wished for – if that were the case a heck of a lot more people would win the lottery every week and we'd all be millionaires!

I think that *realizations* are more important than affirmations. For me, they have two senses. The first is to understand what you have every day and to appreciate it. Mrs Primrose would count her blessings every morning when she woke up, almost like a meditation. It brought her more contentment than a dozen affirmations about how at some point in the future she would have a pot of cash and a toy boy. When you realize how much you already have, it gets harder to demand more from the universe. And if you need to make affirmations at all, why shouldn't they be spiritual ones?

The second sense of realization is even more basic, but it's the first thing you need to ground yourself in the here and now and to begin to rebuild your life after a trauma. You have to understand where you are and what you have to climb out of – the dream stream – instead of blindly wishing for everything to get better.

There's usually an instant when you suddenly see very clearly where you are and how you got there and how you need to move forward. I've seen that moment many times, and each occasion it seems like an incredible, exceptional thing, but I do think it can happen to us all, and wherever we are in life, we all have the ability to pull through. Some people need a medium to help them reach that crucial point, others don't. But you do have to want to move on, to grow, to wake up and smell the karma.

I once asked Effie what had led her to the Spiritualist church and she said she'd had something of a revelation years before. She'd nursed first her mother, then her husband Charlie through long illnesses and when both of them had passed, she fell into what she called a void, a deep pit of depression which sapped her will to live her life. Even her sons, who were grown up and had left home, were unable to talk her out of herself. She said it was like being a zombie and no matter what they said or did to try and encourage her it was as though her body and mind were a ton weight.

When I knew Effie her home was always immaculate and she was up first thing in the morning cleaning the world, but she told me that when she was in the void her house was a tip. It just fell apart around her as she sat in her chair in the living room, thinking of Charlie. She still went out to work cleaning other people's homes and businesses, but in her own kitchen the dishes were piling up and the bins overflowing.

Effie and I used to talk about our 'inner voices' and how we reckoned that they probably weren't spirit guides but a part of ourselves that taught us to trust those real gut instincts when we had them. When she was in the void Effie could barely make out what that inner voice was saying. It seemed too far away for her to hear. She knew it was telling her things and trying to give her directions, but the sound didn't carry into the void.

One day she was sitting in her armchair, unable to even realize if she was asleep or awake, when all of a sudden she heard the loudest voice she'd ever heard, which she described as coming from her belly. '*Live!*' it commanded, and she felt as though she'd just crashed down into the chair from a great height. Her hands were shaking, her whole body reverberating with this great shout. She realized she was crying up from her stomach in great wrenching sobs, crying so violently that it was almost like being sick. She looked around the living room and saw what a sty she was living in, and she was suddenly there in it, not in the void. She said it was like being plugged into a battery, as a burst of energy propelled her out of the chair and into her cleaning cupboard, and she cleaned the house from top to bottom, seeing everything she had to do and focusing intently on one task after another until it was all done and she was standing back in her living room with total clarity.

'From that moment I was back in touch with my inner voice,' she told me, and it was the same voice that led her to the Spiritualist church to practise healing and later to develop her mediumship. That inner voice helped her to do everything right up to the moment she died and, I'm sure, beyond.

It's never too late to come back to your life. No one is a write-off. I remember a woman who used to come to our salon once a week for a shampoo and set who was well into her seventies. She used to talk very openly to us about her day and it'd break your heart to hear it. Her husband used to come in drunk and beat her, had done for all their marriage, and she had a black sense of humour about it.

'The next day he always brings me gold jewellery,' she'd laugh. 'My bedroom looks like the Pharaoh's tomb! It doesn't give me any pleasure, though, because every one of those bits of gold is a souvenir of a beating.'

The police had been called out to her house 100 times and sent away again and her friends had worn themselves out trying to get her to leave him. We used to ask her why she'd never run away, but she wouldn't be drawn. I think she really felt she had nowhere to go. She didn't want to leave the place where she had grown up and we were also beginning to wonder if she was scared that he'd track her down and do something worse. Perhaps she'd lived like that for so long that she couldn't imagine anything different.

One day, however, she came in with a spring in her step and couldn't wait to tell us what had happened. Her husband had been diagnosed with a serious illness and she was seizing her chance to get out and begin living her life, even though she must have been in her mid-seventies by then.

'To heck with it all, I'm leaving,' she told us. 'I've ruined my whole life, but I'm making a fresh start now.'

It takes as much courage to leave a bad marriage with tons of regrets as it does to stick to one and I couldn't believe she was finally brave enough to pack her bags. There was a lot at stake. She was stepping out into the abyss and to be alone suddenly at that age must be frightening, but she sold all the gold and struck out on her own. Just at the point when she was expected to lie down and die next to a man who had bullied her for 50 years, she refused to finish her life that way. As for her husband, he hadn't had to truly think about what he was doing to another human being, but now he was going to have to take on some responsibility for ruining her life.

I often think about her and wonder just how much living she packed in after she left that bully.

One of my favourite stories of a turning point is one which had such a twist that it was hard to imagine that spirit hadn't played a role in plotting it.

We used to hold healing sessions during the evenings at the church and one evening we were joined by a new bloke. At the end we usually shared something we'd experienced during the session, one at a time, but when it came to Billy's turn he took off. I think he felt it was a bit like an AA meeting and he was supposed to give us his story, so he did, and it was perfect.

He'd been born into a fiercely sectarian home where all his family hated Catholics aggressively. It didn't matter what it was, if it was bad, it was Catholic, or the fault of the Catholic Church, or at least that was what his father taught him. All that bile wasn't confined to conversation either. Billy told us how as a teenager he'd wait outside the church schools and beat up the kids when they left, or how he and some others would break into chapels and smash up everything they could lay their hands on.

Then they'd get out their spray paint and scrawl sectarian slogans on the walls.

That was what shaped him and when he married and had kids, he tried to bring them up the same way, only they had the sense to see that it was wrong.

A year or so before he'd showed up in our church he'd been in a sorry state. He'd been drinking heavily and his children had disowned him. All the booze in the world hadn't been able to cure that bigotry and hatred and his body had been packing in and he had found himself literally in the gutter more than once.

One night after he had passed out in the street, blind drunk, he came to in a hospice with two nuns leaning over him. I wonder if he briefly thought his worst nightmare had come true – he'd died and gone to heaven and it was Catholic! What had actually happened was that he'd been taken to a place run by the Catholic Church to help alcoholics and other addicts.

Billy said that he cried for days because those women were so kind through the ugliness of the drying-out process, as he vomited and sweated and raved. It was one thing coming off the alcohol, but coming off the hatred was another thing altogether. Billy's mind was in a whirl. These were the only people who had ever shown him unconditional kindness and understanding in his life, and they were Catholic! They even took him to counselling sessions when he was well enough, and of course those sessions were run by priests!

So Billy was picked up and put back together again by this community of people who didn't care what he'd done in the past but did see that he could become a well person and even a good person in the future. They got him signed up to AA and slowly, with a lot of work, he started to reconnect to life. He took it upon himself to go and visit a lot of the people whose lives he'd made a misery and to apologize, and, big man that he was, he stood there and let them scold him. His daughters came back into his world and he had grandchildren. People who'd known the old Billy for decades barely recognized this new character.

He could have lived out the rest of his days in hatred, in the atmosphere of aggression he'd known all his life, but he took decisions that changed it and he really opened up his soul and found something better inside. For all that he'd raged at Catholics, he'd only been hating himself and destroying himself, but he'd always had the potential to be a good man. All it took was the kindness and generosity of the nuns.

It might sound 'hippyish' to talk about 'finding yourself', but when you do, it is an amazing moment and a great transformation. No wonder Billy couldn't stop telling people about his change. He came to the Spiritualist church for a while after that first night and we knew he was really better when he calmed down and we found out that he was putting in some time helping the organization that had saved him.

I've seen so many people turn their lives around and it's always a wonderful sight. Some people can turn horror into compassion that changes the lives of others, and in so doing, take control of their own fate.

You still have a life, wherever you are – even if you only realize it when you're 90. You're not finished yet!

22

Waking Up from the Dream Stream

You have to understand your karma in order to improve it, although a lot of people only understand what's happened to them in the post-match analysis. Living in the moment will help: it's the only real, true place, after all. I wouldn't say I can sustain that kind of sublime 'being thereness' 100 per cent of the time – everyone needs playtime and to slip into unreality – but I know that when something happens in my life, whether terrible or wonderful, the only place to be is the present. You can't deal with it otherwise; you have to be there and see what's actually going on.

Let's look at an everyday scenario and see how you can be more mindful. We'll think of a strong emotion and how you might arrive at it and how you might avoid it.

Say you are getting the bus into town and someone behind you is impatient and barges past. They snap at you to get out of their way and when you remonstrate you get a filthy look.

At this point you have two choices. One is to see that person's bad attitude as no part of your day – they're just passing through under their own raincloud and they're probably going to stomp around all day being miserable to everyone and hating themselves.

The other option is to take a bit of that raincloud with you through the rest of the day. You think black thoughts for the rest of your bus journey. When you get to work they've run out of coffee, and that's just typical. Then there's been some hitch with your holiday time and you have to go and talk to personnel to make sure it's sorted. By lunchtime, you've decided that it's a bad day. You don't like your sandwich, the person next to you is slurping their tea too loudly and the afternoon is probably going to get even worse. Sure enough, your boss comes over to bring you a piece of work and you look at him as though he's just run over your dog, even though it's a standard thing that needs doing. Back home on the bus you're all held up by a mum who's trying to get a pushchair on at rush hour and as she wrestles with it you mutter away about people who should know better. A trip to the shops leaves you fuming because the girl on your till is being trained and has to ask for the prices of half the stuff in your trolley. By this point, you hate your life and think everyone around you is a moron who has no idea about the stress you're under. You walk through the front door and your partner says, 'How was your day?' 'Don't *you* start!' you growl and start banging the kitchen cupboards and then of course your partner is hurt and you're having a row.

Now, there's a lot of bad karma being generated there, and not even because of the grump on the bus in the morning but because of you. You could have volunteered to get more coffee or to help that mum with her pushchair. You were only delayed a couple of minutes at the supermarket and it's not as though your life runs like a Swiss railway timetable anyway. Your boss was only asking you to do your job, but you acted as if it was an imposition. Irritation is on the point of becoming anger, annoyance becoming aggression.

Step back. You're already in the thick of an argument with your partner and there'll be a point when you know you're about to say something cruel. Now one of the kids has just come in and pressed your last button – are you going to let go and scream and shout or is it easier than you thought to refuse to take that path? Stop now. Don't let a child be an excuse for bad behaviour, or a marital row be a reason to become a bitch.

The following practice was inspired by a talk by the medium Diane Mitchell. It's a meditation that's all about opening up your awareness of where you are and stopping yourself from receding into your head. It's grounded in the here and now but can open up your mind to something much bigger.

A Walking Meditation

Basically, with this meditation, you take control of your body and you walk it. You should always do this in a space that's familiar to you, like a room in your own home or your garden. It's easier if you are undisturbed.

Stand in a good straight-backed position, breathing deeply into the bottom of your lungs, as you would at the start of an ordinary meditation. Keep your shoulders and your neck really relaxed and let your arms hang down by your sides. Let go of any tension in your body, as it'll only distract you.

You don't have to imagine any scenarios or conjure up any memories now. Just take your right foot and concentrate on taking a step and setting it down. Tell yourself what you're doing. Try and block out any thoughts that aren't about this simple movement.

Then step forward with your left foot, doing the same.

Start to walk slowly and mindfully, perhaps in a circular direction. Start out with the tiniest circle and then work up.

At first you will probably only be aware of what you are doing physically, but later you'll start to notice where you've walked before and your awareness will start to open up. You'll notice each blade of grass, or perhaps one in particular, or part of the pattern on your carpet, or some fluff on the floor-boards. As you take control of your body and stop its movement being automatic, your mind begins to notice more.

Every time a different thought comes into your mind, dismiss it and focus again on your slow walk. If you lose focus for a second, go back to concentrating on each step: lift one foot, take it forwards, place it down, lift the other foot and so on. You're driving the vehicle very deliberately.

Everything in that circle you trace will become more and more apparent because you're not allowing yourself to lose brain energy on anything else. You'll notice things in incredible detail. If you're doing this meditation outdoors, you'll be amazed at how crowded that little space around you will seem with objects and movement and sound. You'll have a heightened awareness of everything around you, because you're right in the here and now. Don't drift into the past or start thinking about what you're going to have for supper – give yourself a break from all that. Just focus on the present.

With the walking meditation you become like a mountain climber hundreds of feet up a cliff face: if you think about what you're having for tea instead of where to put your hand next, you're a goner. (And it's safer than mountaineering, but if that works for you, then do it!) It's a nice balance, to have focus on certain things but not others, a 'recreation' in two senses, as you re-create mind energy.

When I got better at the walking meditation I started to do a version of it on my walk to work every morning. It was amazing. I felt that I was seeing every building for the first time, every tree, every patch of grass. I noticed if a drain was blocked or if there were more milk bottles than usual outside a door.

I saw passers-by differently too. The same people would be on my route each day at the same times and I got to know their faces and would think, 'He's wearing a different jacket today' or 'She doesn't look as though she's looking forward to work.' They barely seemed to see me – I think they were in the dream stream, full of worries about their lives. They were walking without thinking, mentally either in the house they'd left behind or already in their workplace, missing out on all the change and life around them. But why waste time trying to get to a future that hasn't begun or dragging yourself back to a past that you can't alter?

Your mind and body should be in one place, sensing what's right there around you. Your subconscious already knows this, even if you try to ignore it. When you're not being honest with yourself, you'll find that your dreams will be frank with you. Perhaps you're deluding yourself that a boyfriend really cares for you and you make up all kinds of justifications to make a cosy version of things, but in your dreams he turns round and tells you you're an idiot. Maybe you think you like your job, but as soon as your eyes close you see yourself galloping a horse out of the office. You wake up in the morning and these dreams seem a bit confusing, so you ignore them – you hit snooze on your mental alarm clock.

I've come across many people whose lives were unfolding in their dreams. I had one friend who was living very much under her mother's thumb but who didn't seem to be able to see that the old woman was manipulating her into staying with her, belittling any new friends she got and undermining any bids she made for freedom. This friend dreamed endlessly of salmon swimming up a stream, leaping out of the water and being caught by her mother, who was standing on the bank with a big net! Believe it or not, she couldn't make the connection between this dream and her mother's treatment of her for ages, but it was a revelation when she did.

Some people choose not to wake up, even when it's not only their subconscious but everyone around them telling them that something's wrong. Is it a fear of failure or is there some destiny drawing them to a bad situation? Maybe we think loved ones or peers will judge us for not having the perfect marriage or job, so we pretend we have, even when we know that we really need to make some changes. In the dream stream we're just cruising along with our fingers in our ears.

There are some people who can be spontaneous about their choices in life and despite this their decisions aren't a wild, reckless gamble but have a calmness to them. If you're already worrying, 'Well, what if I did that and I got it wrong?' then you have to sit down and ask what all this worry is, where it really comes from and what good it does you. If you feel you've already chosen a bad path, then clear an escape route instead of fatalistically deciding that there's no way out. Like Billy, you cannot change the actions you took in the past, but you can learn from them when you step back and look at them with clear eyes. And then look to the future. If you're in tune with life you'll know which is the right path to choose – your whole body will resonate with that decision. Most of us can't do that automatically, but that's to our advantage, because we can stop and think, 'Why am I doing this? Is it the correct thing to do? Am I prepared for the consequences?'

Be present in your life and take your cues from it. You have the power within you to open up a whole new faculty of thinking.

To build your inner strength you need to make your inner world a nicer place, not a dark place haunted by fears of death and pain and emotional hurt. What do I mean by your inner world? It's hard to explain because so many people use that place wrongly. Most people don't understand or trust their inner world; for them, it's the place they go to contemplate fear and worry. Often when we were children that inner space was the place we went to to daydream, but of course as adults we're not supposed to do that, so we fill it up with imaginary horrors instead. If you've ever woken in the early hours of the morning and felt alone, it's because you suddenly had nothing to fall back on but that inner space and it expanded until it felt like the whole world. You couldn't distract yourself from it any more. In the West we fill our lives with music, TV, newspapers, magazines, books and the internet so we don't have to face that space during the waking hours.

Our inner space should be a place where we see the positive. When we learn to think appropriately and navigate through our own minds a little better, it's the part of us that will have a higher, more spiritual function. Turn that space into a good retreat for yourself. Use it as a place to conjure up something you like or to take the sting out of a bad situation. When I was frightened as a child I'd play a kind of mental computer game of tennis. It was neither good nor bad, just something neutral for my brain to do instead of worrying.

A Meditation for an Inner World

In an ideal world, there wouldn't be violence, hatred or suffering of any kind. And if most of us had the power to remove all of this from the world tomorrow, we would.

To remove such things from the world we live in we must first remove them from ourselves. Remembering that the world we live in is filled with suffering and misery will cause us to worry and fear and become angry and hate-filled. Yet when we concentrate on peace, strengthening our mind and building up our inner world, the negativities of the physical world are less likely to affect us. To remain strong in this life we must create a place of peace in the mind, a place where our spiritual nature can grow and lift us above the external world and its pain and struggle.

Go into your meditation and remind yourself that your inner world is peaceful and connected to the divinity of spirit. Tell yourself that no matter what happens in the physical world, your spirit is indestructible and will not be affected. Be at peace with all life and realize that even in the most ignorant of men there lies a divine spirit which has the capacity for love.

This is a place to begin to realize the great difference between the external world with all of its turbulence and the place of stillness where you are now at peace. From this state of inner peace you can begin to build compassion for yourself and for all other beings.

It is only from this inner self that you can truly know and be affected by love.

Be at peace.

Your inner space is the place where you can build up your inner strength, but is this enough to make a difference to the world? There are people who express great strength just by having an immense compassion for others which they channel into prayer. There are others who are at their most formidable when they get out there and do things. I think both those ways of being are appropriate and can balance each other beautifully. You can have an active inner life and address things on a spiritual level, but you can also do something concrete. Once you have arrived at a place of peace and compassion in your own mind, action is often the best way of expressing it. Praying that the shopping is magically done for a bed-bound friend or that their child automatically gets good exam results won't do any good, but you can say, 'I know maths, let me help him with his homework,' or add a few extra items to your own shopping list.

You don't have to go looking for these opportunities, sometimes they'll come to you and all you have to do is recognize them. There's an old Spiritualist hymn that goes, 'If you have a kindness shown, pass it on, pass it on.' So why not work one morning a week at a charity shop, or give blood, or, if you're haunted by the story of an abused child, say, volunteer for ChildLine or raise some cash for the NSPCC or Dr Barnardo's. It beats working yourself up into a fury about the negligence of the social services.

You'll actually need to give something of yourself, plus time and effort, and that's fine, but also remember not to be a martyr to it – you need to live your own life too, not give yourself away. That's where you'll draw the energy to help others.

I remember meeting a man who worked in a soup kitchen in Glasgow with his wife every year at Christmas time. He told me, 'The best thing is, we invite one of these people round to our house on Christmas Day for dinner and then on Boxing Day we have all our family over and we tell them what we've done. That's what makes it really satisfying.' Of course, it went without saying that they didn't invite some old alkie round for dinner the other 364 days of the year!

I met that guy because I was doing hairdressing down at that soup kitchen. A friend of mine who's also called Gordon had suggested it. He was the kind of compassionate person who did a lot for people and would never boast about it. He wasn't under any illusions about it either. It was just part of who he was and the way he'd been brought up. The way he saw it, my trainees from the salon would have a chance to practise cutting hair if we all put in an evening a week down at the soup kitchen and so we'd all get something out of it. I would get my staff trained and the down and outs in the homeless shelter would get a haircut. And the organization running the shelter could say that it had something more to offer their clients, as there was already a dentist and a chiropodist volunteering.

I didn't do it because I thought I'd learn something, but it turned out that I did, it just came with the job. Chatting to those guys taught me a lot about what's really important. We could always go safely home and wash off the smell of the shelter and the lice, but at the back of our minds was the thought, 'There but for the grace of God go I.' They were ordinary guys who had made some bad choices and it hadn't taken much to pitch them out of the everyday world. To be honest, I don't think the haircut actually made any difference to them, but you couldn't buy the stories they told and the reminder that you could drift away without even realizing it and wake up in a place you would never have chosen.

In every story we read in the newspaper or see on the telly there's a moral, a message for us, and it goes beyond:

'Try to avoid natural disasters.' But you don't need to read a book or flip through a newspaper to find these stories – they're there in your everyday life, happening next door to you, or in your workplace, on the street outside your house between the homeless characters you pass on the way to the shops, or even in your own home. There's human drama going on everywhere. There's always someone suffering and, equally, there's always someone striving to overcome that suffering. And if you deal with your own problems and truly help others, you're on your way to really living your life and playing your part to the full in that great human drama.

23

'Can We Ever Be Prepared for Death or Loss?'

One of the reasons it is so hard for us to deal with bereavement is that we've lost sight of the fact that human loss is an intrinsic part of our lives. We try to push it away and not deal with it, and then when a loved one dies or when we ourselves get the worst news from a doctor, we are devastated. But it's a natural part of living in this world. Human bodies are not indestructible, like spirit. You don't have to uncover the mysteries of your destiny to know that we're all going to pass over eventually.

A young friend called Stevie, who was learning to be a healer, asked me to see his uncle, Chrisy, who had just been diagnosed with terminal cancer. After the initial news he had gone downhill rapidly but was trying to be brave for his family's sake. He was staying with Stevie's parents and the young man was worried about approaching him to suggest a healing, because he hadn't admitted that he was doing healing work and he thought his family would think it was all nonsense. He started by just talking gently about healing, trying to bring his uncle round, although I would have understood if Chrisy had had no patience with it. From what I'd heard, there was nothing I could really do for him – the cancer was spreading fast, with tumours in his brain, his lungs, liver, kidneys, lymph nodes... The odd thing was, when I finally saw him I thought he could still have more than the three months predicted by the doctors. He did actually look as though he could die, but from fear, not cancer. I'd seen a lot of people who were close to the end with that disease and he didn't look like them.

Straightaway he wanted to know how he was going to die, and when, and I said why didn't we just concentrate on relaxing his body first – I couldn't promise a cure but I might be able to make things easier. I did my best and as we chatted I asked him a few things.

'Chrisy, did you feel ill before you heard from the doctors?'

'I didn't know I was ill till they told me and then it just took over.'

'How much of how bad you feel is just in your mind?'

'What?'

I tried to explain that I thought he was turning in on himself instead of living.

'If you died next week, Chrisy, what would you have done with those seven days?'

The healing we did in the first session gave me an amazing feeling. Chrisy actually went into a kind of half-conscious state and I had the sense that I usually got when working with a group of mediums who were using trance techniques, of a spirit guide being present who was not my own. I'd never experienced that before in a healing, but I knew it also reaffirmed that Chrisy was going to pass soon. When we're about to pass there's often an attempt by spirit to get close to us and help us prepare.

I didn't speak, but talked mentally or telepathically to the guide, asking for evidence. I thought, 'Lift Chrisy's right hand and turn the palm to face his cheek,' and up it went, into position. 'That's good, you're doing well. Now put it down on his knee, palm up,' and the hand lowered slowly, turned and rested on Chrisy's knee.

All this time spirit was coursing through Chrisy and I was aware that as well as that very evolved spirit guide, he had his family around him. When he came to, he was blown away. 'I ... I just can't work out how to say what it felt like. I'm gobsmacked,' he said, and I knew exactly what he meant. I'd experienced it often enough when a spirit guide came through me. In Chrisy's case it wasn't so much a healing as a sharing of the spirit guide's life with his own, giving him a dose to help him live a little longer.

He had no memory of the telepathy or of moving his arms, but when I told him about his family he was surprised I knew, saying, 'I could feel my mum and my dad and other people all around me. I don't know how, but they were definitely there.'

Afterwards he felt so good that he forgot to take his walking stick with him.

Stevie was obviously delighted and asked me if I thought the healing would save his uncle, but I told him that wasn't the point. What we needed to do was to lift him out of the fear of dying, because that was inevitably coming, and to help him come to terms with it.

I did a few healing sessions for him and we always had great chats afterwards. Stevie helped too. I think that's when he realized for himself that his uncle would pass over, because he too felt the tremendous sense of spirit that was still crowding round the dying man. We couldn't save his life, but we could make the time he had left sing.

Eventually one day Chrisy said to me, 'You know what, Gordon? I am going to live until I die now.'

And so he did – in fact he lived his life so hard that he outlived his diagnosis for nearly nine months. During that time he was at every party, drinking, laughing, loving life, being right in the thick of his family. He didn't get any new drugs, he just had the strength to change his attitude, and what an example he became. You really can live while you're dying.

One night I was having an impromptu party at my house for a friend who had lost someone dear to them and wanted to celebrate their life with what you might call an Irish wake – lots of whisky, tears and laughter. Chrisy dropped by and joined in, and then something really special happened.

I'd been working on a TV series called *Psychic Therapy* and one of the stars who'd appeared on the show was the soul singer Mica Paris. We'd become good friends, but I hadn't realized that Chrisy was an enormous fan of hers. On the night of the wake, the doorbell rang again and of course it was Mica.

Chrisy was gobsmacked and she sat down the sofa with him and they gabbed away about music and growing up in south London like old friends. Later, she sang for him, right there in the living room.

'Gordon,' he said with a grin from ear to ear, 'I don't need a healing today. That was the best thing that's happened to me in years.'

It all came together so beautifully that you had to wonder if spirit had a hand in it all.

Stevie called me a while later. 'Chrisy had to go into hospital last night. I think he's going to pass today. Something's telling me that.'

'Why are you sitting at home?' I asked.

'Chrisy's in a coma,' he said.

'Why are you sitting at home?' I asked again. 'If you don't go to be with him, you'll regret it, because it doesn't matter that he's in a coma, he'll hear you and know you're there. Spirit's put him in that state because he's very near to crossing over now and for him it's like those trances we put him in in the healing sessions. Those were to prepare him for what's happening now. Go and see him.'

Stevie later told me that when he got to the hospital he went straight to his uncle's room and just thought, 'I want to take his hand,' so he sat by his bedside and reached out. 'It was incredible,' he said. 'Chrisy didn't wake up, but his arm just reached out and went round my shoulder and hugged me, as though he could see what he was doing, as though he knew where I was.' They sat for a while like that and Stevie said it was the most peaceful, reassuring experience of his life, a parting gift from his uncle, and he stayed for as long as he could. Chrisy slipped away a little later.

If you can face that darkness as Chrisy did and know that you will pass but find strength in that, you're well on the road to enlightenment.

I remember hearing about a Tibetan Buddhist teacher who was dying of cancer. People asked him why he wasn't worried or frightened, and he replied simply that someone had to take some of the illness out of this world and it might as well be him.

He turned his diagnosis into a way of clearing up the stains of the world. That idea can help the living, too.

They know the dying aren't suffering for nothing; they are taking on the darkness and winning a small victory.

In fact we never stop being a part of spirit. Before we are born into this world we exist in spirit and a part of our consciousness remains there throughout our lives, connecting us to others, whether we're aware of it or not. When we die the rest of our soul simply joins that part in spirit.

Death makes us want the people we have lost more than we ever realized when they were alive. Perhaps it can be a reminder to us to appreciate those we love now and to strengthen the connections we already have, as well as reaching out to those in spirit. It's not that the bond between us is broken when they pass over, but why waste what we have now?

I gave a reading to a woman in her sixties I'll call Jane, who had recently lost her mother. Her husband had died suddenly at a very young age, leaving her with two kids to raise, and when her father passed away, also very suddenly, she'd moved in with her mother to look after her.

She told me she lived her life in greyness – she was out every morning working as a cleaner from six to eight, then home to look after her mother, then out to work again from five to eight and that was her day. Both women were grieving, but the mother took it to an extreme, all but turning herself into an invalid. Her daughter was resentful and they argued constantly for 20 whole years of this miserable existence. The mother used to say that they were cursed, having lost their men so young.

When I gave the reading, the mother came through to her exhausted, angry daughter and said, 'I know about John. I'm glad the curse is lifted now and thank you for doing my hair.'

This transformed her daughter's face. She told me that after those 20 years of misery, her mother had suddenly become genuinely ill with a cancerous tumour and it was as though the whole house woke up. Suddenly the time they had together, which had seemed never-ending, was soon to be cut short, and it changed their relationship. She watched her own children hugging and loving their grandmother and found to her surprise that she wanted to do the same, although after those decades of resentment she didn't know where to start.

But she did, almost when it was too late. Two days before she died, her mother was lying in bed in hospital, her hair a mess, and Jane said, 'Do you want me to do your hair, Mum?' Her mother nodded.

As she stood behind her mother, carefully combing her hair out and winding the rollers on, her mother, without looking round, said, 'You know I've always loved you.'

Jane couldn't speak for the lump in her throat. She felt her mother's shoulders shaking and knew her own were trembling too. She didn't say anything, but in those last two days she sat and held her mother's hand and just spoke to her mentally, repeating, 'I'm so sorry, and I love you and I wish grief had never driven us apart.'

As she thanked me at the end of the reading, she explained that John was the man she had begun to see after her mother had died, because she had told her to go and have a life and break the curse and because she had realized that she didn't want her own children to see her as broken and wretched as their grandmother had been or to hate her the way she'd hated her mother.

We know we'll see our loved ones again in spirit and that they'll still love us when we get there, but in the meantime we should take heart from what we can make of our relationships now. Express your love in the here and now, not the hereafter.

When we make a connection of love to another person and both of us are touched by it at a deep level, that love becomes alive in us and a real part of our existence. It is part of our human self but bigger than we are. It's that love we take to the other side with us when the physical body dies. It's also what we first bring to this life; the newborn's first requirement is to find love. It lives in the heart of us at all times, whether we are aware of it or not.

The episodes, both uplifting and painful, which occur in the course of our lives will usually depend on the actions we perform and how we cope with the consequences. We can try to learn from them and to do better or we can ignore the consequences at our peril and have them repeat until we become aware.

Some events, however, will come from a bigger karma, in which humankind as a whole is affected. Such karmic events are out of our individual control and only acceptance can help us to understand and grow from them.

Our true nature lies in our spiritual evolution, as Chi explains here:

Your human life cycle is reflected in the universe itself. You are born and you die, just as all the while new stars are born in the heavens as old ones die, yet the universe as a whole is still expanding and growing. It does so because of the greater yet more subtle force which shapes and guides it: life.

Living and dying make up only part of life and the same is true of the human world. Men have lived and died since they first arrived on this planet, but the subtle force of consciousness in man has expanded and continues to do so. With each life and death, more darkness will be removed and replaced by enlightenment in the world of man, as in the wider universe each celestial body that implodes and dies drags some of the dark density out of space, allowing space to become lighter.

Life and death will always follow one another as long as they exist in space and time. Humankind is in a constant state of change. The more enlightened we become, the more we will feel the reality and often harshness of our existence until complete understanding is realized of our true selves, or 'spirit', which exists with and above the human emotional self and which lightens when any moment of any human life is truly understood, or when a person passes over.

Those in the physical realm who are void of emotions still have much to learn about their true nature and their journey through life. Those who have travelled further and feel the reality of their existence are on the threshold of a whole new reality.

The universe becomes lighter as time moves through it like an invisible sea being pulled towards a distant shore, and all the life forms which exist in the sea of time will be remembered as part of that universe. Nothing will be forgotten and everything will be made use of as man continues to exist and grow through the dense darkness of ignorance. As time passes, human consciousness will become brighter. This of course means that there will be many more episodes of living and dying.

You may never know when a star or an individual unknown to you has perished, but the effect of that burst of light will reach you on some level, even if it is beyond your reckoning. It is relevant to a deeper part of your being. The parting of one dear to you must be treated in the same way.

When taken personally, it hurts as it moves through your mind and emotions, but be sure that on a higher, more spiritual level, that goodness and light have been born.

There is nothing more to be said...

Afterword

I first met Robert Beer not long after the tragic death of his daughter. I still consider the sitting we had to be one of the strangest, yet deeply spiritual, appointments I have ever made with the spirit world. It would seem that there are still so many things we do not know about our journey.

I consider Robert to be a pioneer of the spiritual journey, and my thoughts and my love are always with him. I'll let him tell the story...

Robert Beer

In 1961 my younger sister Lynne died from hydrocephalus at the age of three. The build-up of fluid on the brain led to a condition where her head grew to weigh more than her body. She was incurable, immovable, cot-bound and emotionally unresponsive to sound and music. She was also a secret our parents kept from the eyes of the world.

The concept of sibling bereavement was not widely acknowledged at this time. Grief over the loss of a child was the legacy of parents, mourning the duty of adults. At

14 I was considered too young to attend her funeral and I came back from school that day to find the lily-scented room where her silent coffin had stood now filled with people talking and drinking sherry, most of whom had never been in our house before.

The secret of Lynne's tragic existence on this Earth was over, the focus of care and dedication needed to maintain her was gone. Other secrets now came to take their place and within the space of two years my parents had separated and found new partners, and by the age of 16 I was homeless and on the road.

This sequence of events would have been traumatic were it not for one strange experience. The night after Lynne died I had a 'dream' in which we were flying together through the deep blue vault of a vast and luminous sky. In the form of a three-year-old she was perfect, with no physical deformity or mental impediments, full of joy, love, intelligence and life. I knew that she had come back to reveal to me the truth of the spirit's continuity into the life after death, and the pristine beauty of this experience has always remained with me. It informed me of everything that I would need to know about grief, loss and love, and the gift of always being open and willing to use this understanding to help others.

The death of a sibling usually causes young people to grow up quickly, but the permutations of anyone's growth are dependent both on destiny and free will. Destiny is 'that which arises'; free will is how we process or deal with what arises. Lynne's 'after-death communication' catapulted me onto a path of intense spiritual enquiry that has unfolded unto this day. The eternal question of 'Why?' confronted me then and I realized that the search for spiritual meaning was the only path really worth following. I was soon drawn to the Gnostic traditions of the East, especially the visionary symbolism of Indo-Tibetan Buddhism, of which I am now considered to be one of the world's leading experts. These esoteric traditions are extremely rich in their philosophical teachings around the 'big questions' of life – birth, suffering, death, transmigration, rebirth and the eternal law of karma, or 'cause and effect', that binds all of these experiences into a meaningful pattern of spiritual evolution which culminates in liberation from the sufferings of *samsara*, or cyclic existence. Some of these ancient doctrines are so profound that many physicists and neuroscientists are now beginning to recognize their true meaning and value. Mind science is rapidly becoming a new religion, with research into the study of consciousness being viewed as the 'final frontier'.

Beyond the confines of monotheism and scientific rationalism, with their deterministic laws of divine redemption and natural selection, the ancient traditions of Buddhism and Hinduism are like a spiritual supermarket where one can freely pick and choose from a staggering array of doctrines and belief systems. All of these doctrines have as their goal the promise of complete liberation from the relentless cycles of death and rebirth, the sufferings of which are perpetuated through our own negative karmas, or 'actions' of thought, word and deed, which are destined to bring future consequences. The concepts of 'sowing and reaping' and 'the deadly sins' are common to most religions, although they have lost most of their potency in the modern world. I have spent my life studying these doctrines, especially those concerned with the psychic techniques used to mimic the experience of death and gain control over the so-called 'intermediate states' experienced between death and rebirth. These visionary states are described in *The Tibetan Book of the Dead*, an enigmatic text that is now widely considered to be the most authoritative manual on the art of dying. But at heart I have always been an unrepentant Spiritualist, for the evidence of things unseen always tends to erode any notion of uncertainty.

In March 2005 our elder daughter Carrina died in a diving accident at the age of 22. She was simply gorgeous, a beautiful young woman full of joy, intelligence, sensitivity and compassion who was training to be a nurse in London. The weekend before her death she had come to visit us in Oxford, where she talked of her fears about her forthcoming diving trip. We tried to dissuade her from going, but the pattern of destiny had been set and somehow there was an inner knowing of what was about to unfold, that inner voice we all must learn to listen to.

And then there was that phone call from the hospital in Devon where they were trying to revive her, that long drive to get there and that precise point on the journey when I knew that she was 'gone'. The rest of that journey was like something I had rehearsed for all of my life, but in the face of death we are poor and inexperienced actors with no masks to hide behind.

And then her sister Rosia and I were together in the room where her body lay, but we were not alone. The presence of her spirit enclosed us, full of beauty, love and peace. Her sanctity was informing us of things sublime, reassuring us that we could be strong, that we could let her spirit fly to the highest point. And then I heard her voice clearly in my mind, saying, 'Dad, you have to contact Gordon Smith.'

For 49 days after Carrina's death I performed the ritual of reading from *The Tibetan Book of the Dead* each night, which is believed to guide the spirit of the deceased to an auspicious rebirth. And throughout all of the traumas of the autopsy, inquest and funeral that follow in the wake of an accidental death, these hours alone communing with what I sensed as the spirit of Carrina were most precious to me.

I had first seen Gordon on the BBC series *Talking to the Dead* in 2004, when, like many others, I had realized what an immaculate gift he possessed. A few months later the day came when Rosia and I were fortunate enough to meet Gordon in London. But his initial remarks were apologetic: he said he felt that something was veiling his clairvoyance and that our journey might have been in vain. After some time it was clear that contact was indeed blocked, so I explained what had happened and our reasons for being there. Then Gordon began to say some things that I cannot easily convey. He used Buddhist terminology, saying that Carrina's consciousness had exited through the crown of her head like a pillar of light, that she had merged with the 'clear light' and had transcended through the realms of the spirit world. He then said that he had never had this kind of experience happen to him before and that he did not know that it was possible. He has repeated these statements to me several times since and I feel that a sense of mystery still remains for both of us.

I feel that this message carried a deep inner meaning for me, like resting in a cloud of unknowing. The question, 'Why did this tragedy happen?' was not really that important. The fact was that it had, and no anger, guilt or what ifs followed in its wake. The question that I really was left with was, 'Where are you, sweetheart, and how can I reach you?'

For those left behind to grieve, the answer is essentially the same. Love is the bridge, and to cross it we have to keep our intelligence white-hot and our grief glistening. Grief comes naturally – that abyss of pain and longing is always just beneath the thin ice of our continuing existence. This is something that we have to learn to live with, something over which we have little choice. The joys of life are easy to receive, but we often accord them little gratitude. But the great tragedies of life we can take either as an insult or a wound, and here I think we do have a choice. The first usually leads to depression, anger, isolation and loss of faith; the second can lead to healing and the dawning of a more beneficial understanding. People often take things as either a blessing or a curse, when it might be wiser to take them as a challenge. Every hunter knows that the most valuable lessons are often the most painful.

But spiritual intelligence does not come naturally, it is something that we have to work at and cultivate. Apparent absence of evidence is not evidence of absence where the subject of life after death is concerned. There is an incredible amount of 'evidence for continuity' that we can now easily access. The clairvoyant skills of gifted mediums such as Gordon can be read about in books or seen on the internet – where we can witness bereaved relatives being granted a 'proof' that can be emotionally uplifting for us all. There is a vast amount of modern and accredited research available on subjects such as near-death experiences (NDEs), after-death communications (ADC), past-life memories and birthmarks carried over by children, deathbed visions recorded by nurses, relatives and hospice workers, memories carried over after organ transplants, out-of-body experiences (OBE), and past-life regression (PLR). None of this research may be accepted as proof by hardened sceptics, but this is not its purpose. For the bereaved, these insights can serve as beacons of light that lead to that 'bridge' to the afterlife. The headstones in every cemetery are full of poignant inscriptions that bear witness to the enduring love and continuity of separated souls who will ultimately be together again. Blind faith is no longer necessary, but spiritual intelligence definitely is.

Three years have now passed since Carrina's death and there have been many levels of change or transformation. I did not imagine that it would be possible to gain such a deep insight into the formless reality of the 'spirit world', but now I know it is. Only time separates us, and the actuality of death is the only certainty that all of us have in life.

Two years ago I came across the work of Dr Michael Newton, who has pioneered research into 'life between lives' therapy (LBL), which involves deep hypnotic regression to access our memories of the 'spirit world'. For if past-life memories are 'real', then so must be the reality of reincarnation, and by inference the reality of the spaces that exist in between lives.

Michael Newton was a traditional hypnotherapist who discovered this technique by accident, and over the course of the past 35 years he has regressed more than 7,000 people into the 'spirit world' and meticulously recorded their experiences. He found that it matters not whether a person is a confirmed atheist or devoutly religious or of any philosophical persuasion in between. For when people enter the deep hypnotic LBL trance that leads from a death in a past life to the threshold of the spirit world, they all undergo similar experiences.

Earlier this year (2009) I underwent two long and separate LBL sessions with a therapist trained by Dr Newton, which were exquisite in their emotional, visual and spiritual content. Most people who undergo this experience realize that the spirit world is our familiar and real 'home' and that we are never actually separate from it, or from our beloved departed who have gone on before us, those whom we cherish and miss. It is that infinite and multidimensional realm of unconditional love, forgiveness, intelligence and joy from which we all manifest and which our 'spirit guides' allow us to glimpse. The experience is sublime. We all appear to be facets of that Divine Source that we call God experiencing itself towards perfection, and there are no hells or religious figures in the spirit world, no divine retribution or Day of Judgement. It is we who must judge ourselves in our own 'life review' of all our thoughts, words and deeds, for every being in the universe instinctively knows the difference between right and wrong.

And there are signs. Recently someone I met briefly after Carrina's death was with a clairvoyant in America and asked if she could tell him anything that would be of help to me. She said: 'Tell Robert that a lady called Rosia was there to greet Carrina when her spirit crossed over and that Carrina remained close to Robert for seven weeks in order to comfort him.' Rosia was the name my younger daughter inherited from her maternal grandmother and seven weeks was the exact duration of my 49-day reading from *The Tibetan Book of the Dead*.

I hope that expressing what I have now come to believe and understand may be of some help to others. Proverbially it is always better to light a candle rather than curse the darkness. There are some lines at the end of the Sam Mendes film *American Beauty* that succinctly convey these sentiments. They are spoken by the main protagonist, played by Kevin Spacey, as his spirit is ascending above his recently murdered body:

I guess I could be pretty pissed off about what happened to me, but it is hard to stay mad when there is so much beauty in this world. Sometimes I feel like I am seeing it all at once, and it's too much. My heart fills up like a balloon that's about to burst, and then I remember to relax and stop trying to hold on to it. And then it flows through me like rain, and then I can't feel anything but gratitude for every moment of my stupid little life. You have no idea what I'm talking about, I'm sure. But don't worry, you will someday.

Also available by Gordon Smith

'The UK's most accurate medium' DAILY MAIL

Gordon Smith
Spirit Messenger

Read Gordon's first book, *Spirit Messenger*, and find out how he became a medium, what has influenced his spiritual development over the years and what it has been like to work with the scientific world. Full of numerous stories told in Gordon's down-to-earth style, *Spirit Messenger* is the beginning of the journey.

Gordon Smith

THE UNBELIEVABLE TRUTH

AS SEEN ON TV

'Hailed as Britain's most accurate medium'
Daily Mail

In this, Gordon's second book, he answers the questions he is most often asked by the people he meets. Gordon explains how the world of spirit works and how spirit communicates; he covers ghosts, hauntings, out-of-body experiences and much more. *The Unbelievable Truth* is ideal for anyone searching for more information on this huge subject area and is a perfect accompaniment to *Through My Eyes* and *Spirit Messenger*.

GORDON
SMITH
Through My Eyes

'Hailed as Britain's most accurate medium'
Daily Mail

FREE DVD

Thousands of people have come to see Gordon seeking healing. From them he has gained a profound insight into the true nature of grief and our relationship with the spirit world. In his third book, join Gordon as he describes the true nature of grief, and how it affects us and our loved ones who have crossed over. An uplifting and insightful book guaranteed to bring peace of mind to anyone who has been touched by loss.

GORDON SMITH

STORIES FROM THE OTHER SIDE

'Hailed as Britain's most accurate medium' *Daily Mail*

This is Gordon's most personal and intimate book to date; in it he shares his experiences of growing up in Glasgow, his development as a medium and his extraordinary life working as a messenger for the spirit world.

GORDON SMITH

'Hailed as the UK's
most accurate
medium'
DAILY MAIL

Life
Changing
Messages

Remarkable stories from the other side

Join Gordon as he inspires and moves you once again.
In *Life-Changing Messages* Gordon allows people to
describe their experiences of his messages in their own
words and talks about how he brings these messages to
people, how they impact him and what he understands
about the nature of the other side.

GORDON SMITH

Hailed as Britain's most
accurate medium ...
The Daily Mail

THE
AMAZING
POWER OF
ANIMALS

There have been many times when Gordon is giving a
reading to a person about the loss of someone very close to
them and the person cannot 'hear' the message – the pain
has closed them down. But when an animal that they know
turns up, the barriers just dissolve and they can accept the
truth of the message that Gordon has given them about
their loved ones. This book is full of astounding stories that
are a great testimony to the power of animals and their
unconditional love for us.

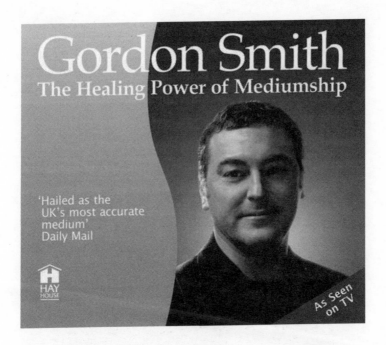

In this fascinating two-CD set, Gordon explains the role of the medium in healing people's grief. The second CD includes meditations to increase your ability to tune in to the spirit world and send absent healing to anyone who is in need.

In this book and CD, let Gordon teach you how to begin to develop your connection with the spirit world and start to form a closer relationship with the spirits that are stepping forward to communicate with you.

Gordon will take you through meditations and exercises that will enable you to experience the difference between psychic ability and mediumship. In his warm and accessible style of teaching, Gordon will encourage you to take the first steps in increasing your spiritual awareness and to begin to trust the truth of your own experiences.

Don't forget you can find out more about Gordon Smith, his life, his work and his upcoming personal appearances by visiting his official website: www.psychicbarber.com

All of the above products are available from all good bookshops or from www.hayhouse.co.uk, or by calling Hay House Publishers on 020 8962 1230

Notes

We hope you enjoyed this Hay House book.
If you would like to receive a free catalogue featuring additional
Hay House books and products, or if you would like information
about the Hay Foundation, please contact:

Hay House UK Ltd
292B Kensal Road • London W10 5BE
Tel: (44) 20 8962 1230; Fax: (44) 20 8962 1239
www.hayhouse.co.uk

***

Published and distributed in the United States of America by:
Hay House, Inc. • PO Box 5100 • Carlsbad, CA 92018-5100
Tel: (1) 760 431 7695 or (1) 800 654 5126;
Fax: (1) 760 431 6948 or (1) 800 650 5115
www.hayhouse.com

***

Published and distributed in Australia by:
Hay House Australia Ltd • 18/36 Ralph Street • Alexandria, NSW 2015
Tel: (61) 2 9669 4299, Fax: (61) 2 9669 4144
www.hayhouse.com.au

***

Published and distributed in the Republic of South Africa by:
Hay House SA (Pty) Ltd • PO Box 990 • Witkoppen 2068
Tel/Fax: (27) 11 467 8904
www.hayhouse.co.za

***

Published and distributed in India by:
Hay House Publishers India • Muskaan Complex • Plot No.3
B-2 • Vasant Kunj • New Delhi - 110 070
Tel: (91) 11 41761620; Fax: (91) 11 41761630
www.hayhouse.co.in

***

Distributed in Canada by:
Raincoast • 9050 Shaughnessy St • Vancouver, BC V6P 6E5
Tel: (1) 604 323 7100
Fax: (1) 604 323 2600

***

Sign up via the Hay House UK website to receive the Hay House
online newsletter and stay informed about what's going on with your
favourite authors. You'll receive bimonthly announcements
about discounts and offers, special events, product highlights,
free excerpts, giveaways, and more!
www.hayhouse.co.uk

HAY HOUSE PUBLISHERS

Your Essential Life Companions

For the most up-to-date
information on the
latest releases, author
appearances and a host
of special offers, visit

www.hayhouse.co.uk

Tune into **www.hayhouseradio.com**
to hear inspiring live radio shows daily!

292B Kensal Rd, London W10 5BE
Tel: 020 8962 1230 Email: info@hayhouse.co.uk